Information technology: agent of change

MURRAY LAVER

Information technology: agent of change

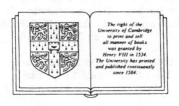

The right of the
University of Cambridge
to print and sell
all manner of books
was granted by
Henry VIII in 1534.
The University has printed
and published continuously
since 1584.

Cambridge University Press
Cambridge
New York   New Rochelle
Melbourne   Sydney

Published by the Press Syndicate of the University of Cambridge
The Pitt Building, Trumpington Street, Cambridge CB2 1RP
32 East 57th Street, New York, NY 10022, USA
10 Stamford Road, Oakleigh, Melbourne 3166, Australia

First published 1989

Printed in Great Britain by
Redwood Burn Limited, Trowbridge, Wiltshire

British Library cataloguing in publication data

Laver, Murray, 1915–
Information technology: agent of change.
1. Society. Effects of technological
development in information systems
I. Title
303.4'83

Library of Congress cataloging in publication data

Laver, F. J. M.
Information technology: agent of change/Murray Laver.
p. cm.
Bibliography: p.
Includes index.
ISBN 0 521 35035 2. ISBN 0 521 35925 2 (pbk.)
1. Information technology – Economic aspects. 2. Technological
innovations – Economic aspects. I. Title. HC79.I55L38 1989 338.4'7004–
dc19 88–21412

ISBN 0 521 35035 2 hard covers
ISBN 0 521 35925 2 paperback

Contents

*

'Change is certain. Progress is not.'

E. H. Carr, *From Napoleon to Stalin, and Other Essays.* M

Contents

'Change is certain. Progress is not.'

E. H. Carr, *From Napoleon to Stalin, and Other Essays*. Macmillan, 1980

1
With our eyes open

Transistors were invented at just the right time for information technology. Offering high reliability and low power consumption, they were immediately attractive to telecommunication engineers and computer designers, and their use surged ahead when it became possible to manufacture thousands of transistor circuits on one small wafer of silicon. Intense competition between suppliers forced them into continuous improvement and, because costs fell sharply with mass production, competition led also to the creation of surplus manufacturing capacity. Producers scrambled to find new markets to absorb their rising output, and few corners of life in Western countries have been left untouched by the silicon chip.

Technological developments of every kind have been so rapid in this century that we have had to accept more changes within our lifetimes than once were spread over many generations. Information technology has helped to force the pace of change in industry, commerce, government and everyday living; but nowhere is development faster than in information technology (IT) itself. Genetic engineering, nuclear energy, and IT have been lumped together as extreme examples of our obsession with 'high technology'. Critics have been moved to speculate whether changes are now coming upon us too rapidly to be accommodated without unacceptable amounts of human and social stress.

Many forecasts of life under IT strive to make our flesh creep at the prospect of a bleak future among the robots in a police state. Journalists know what most of us like to hear: life does become more interesting when there really could be wolves in the woods; and lurid apocalypses are more exciting than the aseptic utopias foreseen by some information scientists. But, 1984 has been postponed: utopia is, literally, nowhere. Certainly the media perform a valuable service by drawing our attention to the unpleasant consequences, for those are apt to escape mention by the promoters of any new project. Yet, we must not sink into a timid neurosis, believing with Ralph Waldo Emerson that 'Things are in the saddle and ride mankind'[23].

Many examples could be cited to show that the consequences of adopting a new technology can ramify to affect men, women and society in ways that were neither intended nor foreseen by the innovators, and which quickly passed beyond their control. IT is proving to be singularly pervasive; its applications press on us all as workers, as citizens and as private persons. But, none of its effects is inevitable; there is no irresistible force, no technological imperative (whatever that may mean). There are, of course, powerful commercial drives, and we must attempt to direct these towards goals that will serve, not use, us.

It would be wise to become well informed before we attempt to decide what is best to do. I am not suggesting that each one of us, electors and members of governments, must dive deeply into the entrails of computers, become expert programmers, or master the mysteries of telecommunications. Knowing how a carburettor worked could not have equipped anyone to predict or regulate the social and economic effects of the internal combusion engine. We must learn enough to challenge and appraise what the experts choose to tell us.

Experts love to wallow in the technicalities of their art, but those among them who aspire to the status and rewards accorded to the members of a profession cannot ignore the wider consequences of their work, unless its applications are trivial or affect only those who are fully aware of what may happen. Neither is true of IT. IT's professionals have a clear duty to inform the public about the powers and the limitations of IT, and to draw attention to whatever consequences they are able to foresee. In doing so in terms that ordinary men and women can understand, they will also deepen and enlarge their own understanding.

Not every expert will welcome that task. Most of IT's professionals are young, tough minded, ambitious, and keen to develop their careers. The judgment of their peers awards no marks for popularizations – quite the reverse. There is also a certain glamour associated with the practice of an esoteric art, one 'not understanded of the people'[11] Older professionals have learnt how easy it is to make a fool of oneself in someone else's subject, and feel that if there are any wider consequences they are best left to some other kind of expert, say to another professional in sociology or human relations. But the problems are upon us and could quite suddenly become too urgent, too late. They are also much too important to be ignored, or to be handled in ignorance or to be left solely to experts of any kind.

The chapters that follow treat their themes in general terms, but where specific examples are used they relate to life in the industralized democracies of North America, Western Europe and Japan. Those are, after all, the places where IT has taken hold but there is a risk of provincialism, of mistaking the local for the universal. Certainly the consequences can be expected to be different in the centralized socialist states, and in Third World countries. Readers should be aware of two other sources of potential bias. The serious discussion of these issues has so far been confined to a few IT professionals and some 'intellectuals', but these constitute a very small self-selected fraction of the population, and are far from typical of the whole. Again, most of the participants have come from Caucasian backgrounds, and cannot pretend to speak for other cultures, not even those of their own increasingly multi-racial societies.

Up to now, IT has been used to speed-up and cheapen existing tasks rather than to make entirely new things possible, although as we move into the possibilities of artificial intelligence that may change. So far, the impact on people and society has been minor. The worries are worries about possible futures, and prediction is an uncertain art. Simple extrapolation from the past works well enough for the near future, for that has been determined largely already by equipment installed and investments made. The planning, development and operation of major systems spans many years, and that introduces a measure of continuity.

Predicting the development of any technology is straightforward compared with attempting to forecast its social, economic and political consequences, because, for the most part, those are the unintended accompaniments of 'progress', and not the deliberately planned results of social engineering. Computers themselves have been recruited to help in working out the longer-term implications by simulations that model our predicament. Yet, in many social and economic analyses the models are little more than descriptions of equilibrium situations. In practice, the most troublesome problems arise from the transient disturbances that are always associated with moving from here to there. Equilibria are rather rare phenomena which receive undue emphasis because they are easy to analyse: real life is one transient after another.

To see beyond the immediate future we need to go behind simple descriptions and the naive extension of trends, and elucidate the causes of change. Here we encounter two severe difficulties which beset all social studies. The first flows from the wide range and variability of human behaviour; the second stems from our ignorance. We just do not know how many causes are operating simultaneously in a given situation, nor can we safely assume that their influences can be independently assessed, for each may inhibit or enhance the actions of others. We rarely know which are relevant in particular circumstances, nor exactly what relations exist between them, nor in what time-scales each operates; and we cannot experiment on real societies in order to find out. The most valuable contribution of computer modelling may well be to provide surrogate societies on which economists and sociologists can experiment to develop and refine their ideas.

The social problems raised by IT are less obtrusively physical than those of some other technologies. The IT industry is not very likely to injure its workers, to destroy amenities or to pollute the environment – although the manufacture of silicon chips has done so. Indeed, noise, pollution and the waste of energy could all be reduced by using IT to replace the conveyance of mail and of human passengers. The other side of that coin is reduced employment in the postal and transport industries. The displacement of labour is the most immediate and certainly the most discussed impact of IT. Unemployment is an economic and social problem that probably requires a political solution, and political and economic power each grow near the sources of information. IT may be used to concentrate those powers, but it could equally well be used to promote a radical decentralization: the choice is open.

I firmly believe that as many of us as are willing to make the effort should equip ourselves with sufficient understanding of IT's immense potential, and its limitations, to be able to take part in reaching the decisions that will shape our future. As Logan Pearsall Smith once wrote: 'Only those who get into scrapes with their eyes open can find the safe way out'[61].

2
The ingredients of IT

Programmed control

Marshal McLuhan could be lured by the prospect of an epigram into uttering a delphic half-truth. Even so, his phrase, 'the medium is the message', does actually fit a large IT system, for its imposing façade confers an undeserved authority on its output. We charitably assume that so much blood, brains and treasure would not have been poured out unless the results commanded our instant and unquestioning acceptance. But it is not quite like that. Computing plus communications is a quite exceptionally powerful combination, and we need to consider why that should be so. For most people, computers are the mysterious part of IT. After more than a century's experience, rapid electrical communications over long distances are taken very much for granted.

With the widespread use of personal computers, everyone now knows that 'hardware' is the electronic and mechanical equipment, and 'software' the controlling programs which make it do what we require. Interchangeable control is not a particularly new idea. The drive mechanisms, electronics and loudspeakers of a record player are the hardware of a general-purpose musical instrument which can simulate a symphony orchestra or a soprano by playing the corresponding record. Records are easily changed, and there is no limit to the number of different ones that can be played. It is the same with computers and their programs.

The analogy is worth pursuing a little further. We can reproduce a particular piece of music only if we can buy, borrow or steal the right record. If no one has yet recorded it then we cannot hear it; and a special recording cannot be organized in an instant or at low cost. With computer programs also, those of significant size or merit cannot be produced quickly or cheaply; and those prepared by the imperfectly skilled can be no less clumsy and prone to errors than the effusions of amateur musicians.

Hardware and software are to some extent interchangeable. Schubert's *Trout Quintet* could be reproduced either by a specially designed musical box or by playing the appropriate record. Similarly, a computer can be constructed with hardware designed to perform just one task, but most have general-purpose hardware which we can program. Special-purpose hardware is fast and reliable, but expensive and inflexible; it is used where absolute dependability is more important than versatility – say for controlling a chemical plant or a power station. It can be given some measure of adaptability by providing easy ways to alter the connections in its control wiring. The program is then said to be 'hard-wired', or (but most regrettably) it may be described as 'firmware', being neither absolutely hard nor totally soft. There is no limit to the number of different tasks that a computer can be programmed to perform; its range is open-ended but not unbounded. It is this combination of general-purpose hardware with interchangeable special-purpose software that gives computers their power and versatility.

The software may be special-purpose but it does adapt its control to particular circumstances arising when it is executed. It does this by means of 'conditional jump' instructions, which enable the computer to respond suitably depending on which of two alternative conditions is met. Thus, a payroll program needs to suit its calculations to individual employees: is he sick? has she worked overtime? have they had a baby? Conditional-jump instructions take the form 'If A is the case, then do B; otherwise do C'. When used by a skilful programmer they add enormously to the appropriateness of a program's response to foreseen, but as yet undetermined, conditions as these are signalled by the input data. This sensitive response of a generalized program to particular circumstances was provided in Charles Babbage's original design of 1832.

Hardware

Computer hardware consists of electronic circuits formed on thin wafers (chips) of very pure silicon by an elaborate sequence of processes which includes photoprinting, etching and vapour deposition. The details concern only a very few specialists, but the results have important implications for us all. First, when they are mass-produced silicon chips are very cheap. Second, although a single chip carries many thousands of transistors and other electrical components with all the connecting 'wiring', it is less than 10 mm square and less than 0.1 mm thick. Third, they work at extremely high speeds, tens of millions of operations a second is not unusual. Fourth, they are extraordinarily reliable, in part because they are too small to be shaken to pieces by vibration or mishandling. Their combination of high speed with high reliability means that, in its working lifetime, a chip will execute thousands of billions of operations without error, far, far more than any other kind of machine we have ever made.

A silicon chip carries a large number of small electronic switches, commonly called 'gates', which are interconnected to form a complex network of paths through which brief electrical pulses stream at high speed. These pulses are bunched and spaced into clusters which we use to represent numerals, letters or other symbols according to some pre-arranged code. By opening or closing particular gates the pulse streams are directed to interact, to combine or to oppose one another, in order to generate consequent streams that flow out of the network. That is *all* that the hardware does. It does not in some mysterious way 'do arithmetic' any more than the movement of beads along the wires of an abacus does arithmetic. In both cases we design the machines and operate them according to rules that mimic the operation of the rules of arithmetic. When we use the pulse groups to represent letters or some other kind of non-numerical symbol the operations parallel those of logic rather than those of arithmetic –

for example, comparisons to ascertain whether two pulse groups contain elements that are identical or different.

The costs of computer electronics have been plummeting at some 30% per annum over the last two decades, and seem set to continue doing so for at least another 10 years. These falling costs, plus the need for mass-production to sustain their fall, have been the principal causes of the recent rapid expansion of IT, especially for domestic use. There is no sign that IT's hardware is anywhere near the peak of its achievable performance. One limit is set by the fact that electrical pulses cannot travel between gates faster than the speed of light. Another is set by the rate at which those gates can open and shut, which depends on the movement of electrons through semi-conducting materials. Attempting to offset those limitations is one reason why silicon chips are made so small, and plenty of scope remains for further miniaturization. Moreover, only two-dimensional arrays of components have been used so far and opening up the third dimension will greatly increase the number of components that can be crammed into ever-smaller compass.

Up to now, most computers have been designed for 'serial processing', which means that they plod through their programs step-by-step. Designers are at last developing the techniques of 'parallel processing' in which several units work together on the separable parts of a single problem. Not all problems can be split into non-interacting parallel streams, but groups of several hundreds of cooperating computing elements are being applied to those that can. IT systems that could be programmed to recognize specified patterns would be invaluable in science and in industry: and they would find many military applications. Pattern recognition, also called 'image processing', is one of those functions that can be performed most effectively by arrays of cooperating elements. Without doubt we shall see very significant developments in all aspects of parallel processing; indeed, we have almost everything to learn about it, and its development is heavily funded. With continued miniaturization, and the falling costs of microelectronics, it is very safe to predict that IT will advance further in the next 10 years than in the whole of its past.

Various electro-mechanical machines are associated with a computer's electronics. Keyboards enable our fingers to enter input data and commands, and some systems can be spoken to in a vocabulary of a few thousand words; loudspeakers answer us back, video screens display and printers record the output of results. Magnetic tapes and magnetic or optical discs act as data stores which record, retain and on demand rapidly replay files of data previously entered, or recorded as the results of previous processing.

Computer suppliers delight in parading figures that are intended to amaze and impress us with the incomparable speeds and unmatched storage capacities of their own splendid hardware. This computer can perform several hundred millions of additions each second, that optical disc can store a thousand pages of typescript and recover any sentence in a small fraction of a second. Most such numbers are pure puffery. Even so, we can use one of them to show why computers can be expected to bear more heavily on men, women and on society than did slide rules or adding machines. A fast computer can add or subtract pairs of 10-digit numbers at the rate of 150 millions of operations a second, and that is about three thousand million times faster than you or I. In about one-tenth of a second it can do as much raw arithmetic as you or I could do in our entire working lives, and not make a single mistake. Moreover, the answers would be immediately available instead of after 40 years of laborious toil, and at a cost of less than a penny compared with our life's wages of half a million pounds or more. We are, of course, employed to do much more than simple arithmetic. It is, nevertheless, surprising and somewhat humbling to discover how many human tasks can, by taking thought, be boiled down to a routine sequence of elementary operations. The sequence may be an extremely long one, but a computer will zip through it uncomplainingly, indeed uncomprehendingly; at millions of unit operations a second it gets there long before we do.

However, the high speeds of the machines we have, and the further advances in prospect, must not mislead us into supposing that every problem lies within the range of rapid computation. There is, for instance, the dreaded 'combinatorial explosion', which is easily illustrated by a trivial example. A salesman who has to visit several towns wishes to discover the shortest route that passes through each town once only and returns to the starting point. A computer can be programmed to calculate the lengths of all possible permutations of routes and compare them to select the shortest. That brute-force method works well for four or five towns, but for ten towns the number of permutations has soared above three millions. Even at the highly optimistic rate of a thousand million comparisons a second, routes through 20 towns would require almost 80 years of continuous calculation, and for 30 towns the time increases to millions of years. Arithmetic is not always adequate, and in many cases we are forced to think. Needless to say, this problem never bothers any real salesman.

Software

The importance of software can hardly be overstated; what a computer does, and how well it does it, depends almost entirely on the accuracy and effectiveness of its programs. Yet software is elusive stuff; in its active role when actually controlling a computer it is invisible and intangible to its users. They are quite unable to observe what it is doing, and can infer only what it actually *has* done by noting and analysing the results produced under its control. Just as a musical composition is a set of ideas for sequences and patterns of sounds, so a computer program is a set of ideas for sequences and patterns of arithmetical and logical operations. The music or the program takes a physical form only when its composer writes it down for others to read or use. To control a record player or a computer, recordings are acquired, but these are just convenient copies, they are not themselves the 'intellectual property', the ideas, which are the essence of the program or the music. This somewhat metaphysical digression into the nature of software has very practical implications for its protection against pirating by sneaky scribes. A cynic has said: 'Hardware is what you buy: software is what you copy'

The first computers came without software frills, and their users wrote programs directly in the bleak numerical form of the coded orders which controlled them. Programs in that 'machine-code' are suffocatingly tedious lists which specify tiny-step by tiny-step absolutely every action of the machine. To see a program in machine code is to see at once the often forgotten fact that computers are not at all like us. The use of computers would undoubtedly have been confined to a small handful of enthusiasts if programming had not been made more accessible to accountants, engineers and others whose prime interests lay elsewhere.

The first move was to develop a group of standard programs (standard for one model of computer, that is) which would make computers easier and more pleasant to use. Such a set of programs, now called the computer's 'operating system', controls the input of data, their sorting and storing in orderly files, their subsequent retrieval on demand, and the output of results. It also allows users to write programs in terms that are closer to those they customarily use – for instance, in COBOL for business applications, or in ALGOL for mathematics. Programs in one of these 'high level' languages, and there are hundreds of them, have to be transformed into the machine code of a particular computer before they can control it. That is done in a preliminary process by the computer itself. When the program is a short one, or is to be used only a few times, it can be transformed step-by-step by an 'interpreter' program each time it is run. Other programs are usually transformed once and for all by a 'compiler', and the compiled result is then stored for future use.

It is important to appreciate that computer programs differ very greatly in length and complexity. The program for a straightforward scientific or statistical calculation may contain fewer than a hundred instructions. That for a major commercial application may require a 'suite' of programs to cover a range of related functions and services, and the whole can amount to some hundreds of thousands of instructions. The operating systems of some large IT installations contain more than a million instructions. Writing programs as long as those is a massive task, neither quick nor cheap, and many attempts have been made to increase the productivity of programmers. Some advances have been made, but compared with the dramatic improvement of hardware they are trivial, and the high costs of programming have long threatened to dominate the economics of proposals for new

IT systems. This has stimulated the production of standardized 'package' programs available off the shelf for many common applications. To keep their prices low it is necessary to appeal to the widest market, hence packages require their users to adapt to their ways, and to forgo all others. Packages are standard solutions in search of standard problems. Before using a package it is necessary to examine the principles and procedures on which it is based in order to evaluate their appropriateness, and their limitations. Otherwise we fly blind, processing our data with little knowledge or understanding of how it is being manipulated.

Preparing a large suite of programs can occupy 100 or 200 programmers for two or three years, and no project of that magnitude is completed without error. Software errors are of three main kinds: errors of conception, where the programmer has failed to grasp or to meet the user's requirement; errors of logic; and errors where an instruction has been expressed incorrectly and does not satisfy the arbitrary rules of spelling and syntax imposed by the operating system's compiler. Logical proof that a program is accurate requires it to have been written in a rigorously formal fashion. Proof is simply not feasible for the lengthy programs needed by businesses and governments. After a year or two, most such programs have suffered *ad hoc* patching, extension or amendment by a succession of programmers working a five-day week with varying degrees of competence, and under less than perfect management.

Discovering and correcting errors in programs, named 'debugging', is an exacting task. Residual errors can lurk undetected in obscure corners of a program which provide for rare combinations of data or circumstances that may never happen to arise during its entire working life. In practice, no program that is large enough to be useful can be guaranteed to be free from error; the most we can hope for is that each of those we have found has been corrected – without introducing further errors.

The design of interpreter and compiler programs exerts a strong influence on the execution of a user's work. Any compiler cramps the language it is able to transform by restricting it to a minute vocabulary and a rigidly artificial syntax. In such ways an operating system limits what we are able to do, and constrains or distorts the way we do it. Critics with a melancholy cast of mind see this as yet another example of machines forcing us to adapt to their ways. That sounds ominous until we reflect that even a hammer forces us to hold it by one end and hit with the other.

A computer's operating system is by far the most important part of its software. It determines the face and the features presented to the operators and programmers. It allows the hardware to switch extremely rapidly between several different programs, interleaving their demands and ensuring that errors arising during the execution of one program do not endanger the working of the others. Under its control, several hundreds of users can be connected to one computer and be served concurrently, with each having the impression that she or he has the exclusive use of all facilities. Some of these users may be at the far ends of long telecommunication links; the operating system manages the connections and ensures that errors and failures on any link are detected and handled appropriately.

High-level programming languages are still very far from the unruly, discursive, vague and ambiguous forms of speech we use among ourselves. Nor are most of us accustomed to analysing our work in the minute and exhaustive detail that is necessary before we can program a machine to do it for us. Computers are tiresomely literal-minded beasts, and what they have not been explicitly instructed to do by their programs they do not do. For major applications in business and public administration professional specialists are usually employed to analyse and reconstruct the work to make it more amenable to computer operation, and then to program it. Often they are young men and women who have had no direct acquaintance with the work they program, and who have not lived long enough to have had much experience of anything outside computing. Necessarily they base their system designs on their clients' specifications of requirements, which if they are prudent they will supplement by talking to those currently performing the work.

Those who are attracted to computer work tend to have logical minds and what Liam Hudson has called 'convergent personalities'[34], and their interpretations of their clients' wishes have too often produced rather mechanistic systems. These assume that the men and women who will provide the input data, operate the equipment and respond to the output will invariably do all those things with unfailing accuracy according to rigidly specified formats, sequences and timings. Inadequate allowances are made for lassitude, for occasional lapses of attention, for distraction by the casual exchanges of gossip which bind a workforce together, or for that variation in pace we all find necessary and congenial.

Unsurprisingly, those concerned sometimes feel that the system is using them, rather than vice versa. That unfortunate outcome is not the result of malevolence, or even incompetence. It happened because the computer professionals have, quite properly, sought to advance their client's interest, and to maintain their own competitive advantage. A mechanistic system is cheaper and quicker to design, produce and install than one that deals more sympathetically with human frailty. It is also cheaper and more efficient to run on that narrow, short-term, view of efficiency which saves capital and running costs, but which may well lose in effectiveness by ignoring customer satisfaction and staff morale. The problems associated with program rigidity are even more acute when standard packages are employed. But rigidity and its unwelcome consequences are not an inescapable concomitant of using IT; they result from narrow specialization, plus too hot a pursuit of economy and machine efficiency. Computers can be programmed to work in as flexible and individual a fashion as we have the wit to provide and the wisdom to require.

In its passive form, a computer program consists of a record, usually on a magnetic tape or disc, of a list of letters and numerals. When it is to be used, the operating system first causes the program to be taken in as if it were data and held in the computer's store, it then transfers control to it. In active use, the program is very much like the data it is processing. It is, of course, treated as data by the operating system and processed by it when it is being interpreted or compiled. A program can also operate on itself; that is, certain parts of a program can command other parts of it to be processed in order to modify what they do, or to adapt them to current circumstances. This somewhat strange procedure is of the greatest importance. Its most straightforward use is to enable a given piece of program to be applied over and over again to successive items of data in a file. Otherwise, we would have to copy the same instructions out in full again and again for each item. Not only would that be intolerably laborious, it would be prone to error, the program would be very much longer and it would waste valuable space in the computer's store. By modifying a few of its own instructions, the program is able to reapply the same sequence of instructions to the next item of data, and it repeats this looping-around action until a marker in the data indicates that the last item has been processed. Self-modification opens up many interesting possibilities of which quasi-intelligent activity is probably the one that most puzzles and alarms ordinary men and women.

Artificial intelligence

Ada Augusta, Countess of Lovelace, once noted that a computer 'can do whatever we know how to order it to perform'[1]. Writing in 1842, she was referring to Charles Babbage's Analytical Engine, but her observations apply with equal force to today's 'computing engines'. She makes the astonishingly bold claim 'whatever', for she had realized just how versatile Babbage's engine would be. But, when 'whatever' is qualified by 'we know how' then its range shrinks pitifully in the face of our ignorance. For example, we do not know how, in the meticulous detail required to program it, we ourselves recognize patterns, nor how we lift those that interest us out of a background that does not[31]. That is a more troublesome limitation than it might appear to be, for much of what we do, from scientific research to recognizing our friends or from economic forecasting to reading different type fonts, depends on the identification and comparison of patterns in time or space, or both.

Ada's Limitation, as we might call it, bears on the much discussed and currently topical subject of 'artificial' or 'machine intelligence'[10, 47, 66, 69]. Shall we ever be able to program a computer to produce results which we cannot ourselves achieve, and may not even understand? The inference is that the machine would have altered beyond recognition the program we originally provided, doing so in the light of its input data, its intermediate results and some task that we had set it to perform, but which we knew no specific way of completing. In short, could the machine under the initial control of our program operate in a 'creative' and exploratory fashion and 'learn' as it goes? The scare quotes around 'creative' and 'learn' are intended as warnings that these terms are being applied to actions which produce results that we would call the results of creativity or learning if performed by human beings. There is absolutely no implication that the processes are identical, or even similar, in men, women and computers. Even if they were we would not know, for we have next to no understanding of how we ourselves perform them. These and other oblique references to human behaviour are no more than analogical, but they tend to beg the very questions under examination.

Recourse to Ada's Limitation suggests that if we do not know how to do something then we cannot program a computer to do it either. But, suppose we discovered how to write learning or exploratory programs. Could not they then process themselves and develop in ways that we cannot readily foresee? Eventually, perhaps, that we cannot even understand? A teasing analogy is with a mathematics teacher whose pupil progresses to a level well beyond the teacher's comprehension; but pupils and teachers are human beings and not machines – except to a mechanistic philosopher. Some early work naively assumed that a large store of data, plus programs to interrogate it and to acquire new data, would be a satisfactory recipe for artificial intelligence. The poverty of that approach was exposed when attempts were made to develop machine translation.

Ordinary discourse is characterized by vagueness, incompleteness, ambiguity, unruliness and implicit reference to that vast store of everyday knowledge we call common sense. Again, to translate into French an ambiguous English phrase such as 'That was a fine spring', a program needs to discover the appropriate context in order to distinguish between the season, an athlete's leap, an engineering component and a source of water. So, of course, would a human translator; but context is rarely a problem for us. Human languages and those who speak or write them each have their own idiosyncracies and ambiguities, their own different penumbras of meanings and partial synonyms, and their own tacit references to a complex cultural background – both intellectual and everyday. It soon appeared that translation was as difficult and unsatisfactory as literary critics had always said it was.

Another early ambition of the pioneers was to write a program for playing chess. Once again, it was hoped that a computer's ability to store immense amounts of data and to retrieve them rapidly would suffice, but it does not: the number of moves and countermoves is so large that even the fastest computer cannot make an exhaustive search and evaluation over a useful number of moves ahead, nor would such a brute force approach have deserved the name 'intelligent' anyway. Today's quite successful chess-playing programs mimic the tactical and strategic moves that the best human players have found to be successful.

Chess programs were early examples of what are now called 'expert systems', or even 'intelligent knowledge-based systems'. Accepting that the quest for general intelligence may be like that for the Holy Grail, these have adopted the more modest aim of absorbing and applying the accumulated knowledge of the experts in some limited field. Thus, medical diagnosis of particular groups of diseases has yielded encouraging results. Work on these systems has also revealed the difficulty of extracting expertise from experts, not because they are reluctant to disgorge but because so much of their knowledge is intuitive, and resides below the threshold of deliberate decision or conscious thought. In despair, some programmers have consulted the less-expert experts who have to think more explicitly when practising their art. The problems of winning acceptance by professionals and their clients have also begun to emerge. An expert system must be able to 'explain' the data and methods it has used to reach the results presented. It would be irresponsible to accept them otherwise, for a user may readily assume that the system has taken account of more factors than it has been programmed to hold in its store. Human expertise encompasses much more than a tool-kit. An expert has to understand the limitations of the available data and techniques, and to know when a given method is relevant, reliable and accurate – and when it is not. The uncritical use of clever tricks is a mark of shallowness; and even human experts vary considerably in depth, and even more in breadth of vision.

When it became evident that the development of artificial intelligence was less straightforward than its more optimistic proponents had expected, the subject languished for a while. In Britain, an eminent mathematician reported that the whole thing was a mirage and should be abandoned. History does occasionally repeat itself, and the Lighthill Report[39] did for artificial intelligence what an equally uncomprehending report by Airy[2] had done for Charles Babbage's machine more than a century earlier. In each case government support fell away. Both examples illustrate Arthur Clarke's Third Law that when an eminent elderly scientist says that something cannot be done he is almost certainly wrong, especially when speaking about a field that is not exactly his own.

Artificial intelligence has now returned to fashion. In Japan, a major national project aims to produce a so-called 'Fifth Generation Computer'. The generations of computers are conceived purely for promotional purposes: their function is to attract funds by implying that some significant advance is in prospect which will make the current generation obsolete and unsaleable. The Japanese project seeks to harness both parallel processing and artificial intelligence to the accumulation and application of knowledge, and to the control of industrial robots. The American government has heavily funded the development of computers since the earliest days, principally with the aim of strengthening US military power. Some see artificial intelligence as a way of increasing the complexity of weapon systems in the hope that this will increase their effectiveness, and American work on IT is dominated by the aspirations of the Department of Defense.

The social and human implications of robotics and defence are taken up in later chapters. Here we will touch only on what could prove to be the most profound consequence of work on artificial intelligence, namely its effect in leading us to see ourselves as data-processing machines. We could drift into accepting this false and gloomy view by the slipshod use of such anthropomorphic terms as 'memory' and 'language'. These are mere convenience words, and should carry a government mental health warning that their heedless use can damage your clarity of thought. At best, they express crude and partial analogies.

A computer's 'memory' is no more than the part of its hardware used to store data. We do not refer to four-drawer filing cabinets as an office's memory, and when speaking of computers it is better to use the neutral word 'store' to avoid the misleading overtones resonated by the implied similarity to our own memories. The analogy is not all that useful in any case, for we know much more about the design and use of computer stores than we do about human memory. Again, 'language' is a wildly honorific title for the mnemonic and other easier-to-use coding schemes which we use to declare the instructions we intend a computer to obey. Their impoverished vocabularies and stilted syntax do not remotely approach the rich and subtle complexity of human languages. It is precisely because they *are* so limited, and designed to be unambiguous, that simple mechanical transformations can convert statements in them into their equivalents in some machine code. But that is mere code-to-code conversion, and it would be foolish to expect it to throw a useful light on the problems of translation between natural languages.

The most dangerous of these anthropomorphisms is the hijacking of the word 'intelligence'. Scientists of all kinds have always taken over words in everyday use and given them precise, specialized meanings – energy and (electric) current for instance. Usually this does not matter too much, for the scientific usage is confined to professionals and does not impinge on ordinary men and women. 'Intelligence', however, is a subtly potent word, and it is essential to realize that 'artificial-intelligence' is really just one word. The adjective severely limits the noun and converts the combination into a term of art. Abbreviations are a great nuisance, and often a sign of packaged thinking, but the regular use of the abbreviation AI can help to preserve us from devaluing human intelligence and thinking of ourselves as machines. Were that to happen, it could lead to others treating us as interchangeable human modules (as mere 'homods') which can be plugged-in at will to whatever systems they may devise to further their economic or political ambitions. We are not in the business of competing with IT: it is a tool we may choose to use.

Telecommunications

To convey information, telecommunication engineers use two principal techniques – digital and analogue. Modern telecommunications began digitally with the invention of the electric telegraph, in which pulses of current were sent along a wire according to a prearranged code. Morse's code used different combinations of short and long pulses (dots and dashes) to stand for different letters and numerals. Alexander Graham Bell's telephone, however, used a microphone to vary the strength of the transmitted electric current in a way that mirrored the sound waves and formed an electrical analogue of the speaker's voice. The greater convenience of the telephone led eventually to the decline of telegraphy, and of digital signalling.

All telecommunication signals grow weaker as they travel and have to be refreshed. Electronic amplifiers can be used to restore the strength of the telephone's analogue signals, but they are conveyed by a electric current – a stream of electrons flowing through the wires – and an inescapable randomness in the movements of electrons introduces electrical 'noise'. Interfering signals are picked up along the way. The noise and the interference are also amplified and at each successive amplification they accumulate and gain on the signal until eventually further amplification is useless. Digital signals also pick up electrical disturbances as they travel. However, it is necessary only to determine whether a pulse is present or not, and that can be done in the presence of a great deal of noise and interference. The received pulses can then trigger an electronic device to produce exact replicas of their former selves for onward transmission. This process of 'regeneration' yields brand-new signals free from all disturbances, and digital signals can be regenerated almost indefinitely. Hence, they can be carried over great distances, as communications from interplanetary probes have amply demonstrated.

Ingenious and rather complex electronics enable us to convert speech and television pictures into digital signals, and so to share in the advantages of regeneration. Moreover, the silicon chips developed for computers work best with digital signals, and are now much used in telecommunications also. They are especially well suited for handling communications between computers, for computer data is already in digital form. Computing techniques have entered telecommunications in other ways. Severe interference or faulty equipment can introduce errors, but extra 'check digits' can be added before transmission and examined after receipt to determine whether the message has been corrupted. When errors are detected, the message is repeated automatically, or, by using a larger number of checking digits, errors can be corrected automatically on receipt.

Data signals can also be protected against wire-tapping by coding them in ways known only to authorized recipients. Specialized chips are available which perform complex cryptographic ciphering and deciphering entirely automatically under the control of a hard-wired program built into their design. Computing techniques are used in electronic exchanges which route digital signals through silicon gates rather than electromechanical switches. Also, data messages are being handled by electronic equivalents of the postal service known as 'store-and-forward' or 'packet-switching' systems. In these, the message passes through a series of forwarding stations where computers examine the digits that indicate the destination address, and hold the message in store until the next onward link is free. Intermediate storing and forwarding is repeated several times but so rapidly that users should be unaware that they have not had the exclusive use of a direct link. The object of this seemingly elaborate procedure is to reduce the costs of transmission by enabling many users to share the same links.

For many years, telecommunication systems were state monoplies – or commercial near-monoplies – and they carried only telegraph and telephone signals. The absence of competition, and the undemanding nature of the signals, allowed their technology to evolve at a leisurely pace. Then they were asked to relay television programmes, and later to convey data messages between computers. Those requirements posed much more difficult technical problems which, combined with the introduction of competition, has forced the pace of development. The technologies of telecommunications and of computing converged and have coalesced. One consequence is that the telecommunications element of IT is now advancing at the rapid – and occasionally frantic – pace which has been a characteristic of computing.

An indirect, but essential, use of computing techniques in telecommunications is for controlling the launch of communication satellites, whose injection into orbit requires the utmost precision. The law of gravity requires these 'geostationary' satellites to fly at the height of 36 000 km and the time required for radio waves to travel to and from the satellite introduces a delay of 0.25 s. That delay can be troublesome for telephony when more than one satellite link is employed, although it is acceptable in other applications. The delay and the cost are the same for any two points served by a given satellite, which allows users to site their installations at will, without being constrained by their national networks.

Satellites have particular value for underdeveloped countries with inadequate telecommunication systems, and for serving ships and aircraft. It is arguable that they should be reserved for such purposes, and not squandered on relaying ever-more television channels carrying programs of ever-diminishing merit between the rich nations of the West. Only one geostationary orbit exists (at one particular height above the equator), and only certain parts of the radio spectrum are suitable for satellite use. Hence we are dealing with a finite natural resource which we ought to exploit economically, and equitably between the nations.

Services to road and rail vehicles are becoming important. In countries with established telecommunication systems these services are provided by linking the vehicle to the national cable network through an array of low-power radio stations, each covering a limited area or 'cell'. Adjacent cells overlap and connection is transferred automatically from cell to cell as the vehicle

moves. This 'cellular radio' technique was developed for telephone users, but it is being employed increasingly by businessmen to link their portable 'lap-top computers' into public
databanks or their company's main network.

Until the mid 1980s, telecommunications exclusively employed
electrical signals transmitted through copper wires or carried by
radio waves. The development of lasers and optical fibres has
added the use of light waves. Light is itself an electromagnetic
wave, essentially similar to radio waves but with a very much
higher frequency, and its technology is optical rather than electronic. A single hair-like thread of special glass can replace a pair
of copper wires and serve not only the telephone but also several
independent data and television channels. Optical fibres can be
used over long or short distances, and can replace submarine
cables for international communications. As compared with satellites, they consume no natural resource which is at all scarce,
and their signals cannot be intercepted easily by a malevolent, or
idly curious, eavesdropper: but they do, of course, require an
optical-fibre cable to be laid to every location served.

The marriage of telecommunications and computers has stimulated the development of a range of so-called 'value-added' functions. Among the first of these were 'videotex' services, which
take two forms. One-way services of 'teletext', such as Britain's
Oracle or *Ceefax*, present standardized displays of news, information and advertising on domestic television screens. Two-way
'viewdata' services, such as British Telecom's *Prestel*, allow their
users to interact with the system and make selective enquiries of
large databases; and they could be extended without difficulty to
offer a wide range of computing facilities to supplement a user's
own microcomputer. There is no obvious limit to the range of
value-added services which could be provided: market research
and designer ingenuity will undoubtedly create and satisfy whatever as yet undreamt-of desires can be stimulated in an affluent
society.

Postscript

Some may be disappointed, others relieved, that I have said next
to nothing about the details of electronic circuitry or the curi-

osities of binary arithmetic. Those specialist subjects have no particular bearing on the consequences that may flow from our use of IT. Charles Babbage's Analytical Engine used a clockwork mechanism driven by falling weights; the machines of the 1950s used thermionic valves; today's use silicon chips; tomorrow's may replace silicon with gallium arsenide and the day-after's use optical devices. Yesterday's telecommunications used thick copper wires or erratic shortwave radio; today's bounce microwaves off artificial satellites and shoot laser beams through fine glass fibres; and tomorrow's – who knows? It would be silly to suggest that the details of technology have no significance; they do determine the economics of IT and the range and depth of its application, and thus its potential effects on men, women and societies. But the principles are more important and they do not change.

Computers have achieved notable successes in handling numerical data by programmed procedures, it was after all what they were invented to do. But success in that narrow field should not mislead us into believing that we will be able to apply them with equal advantage to all other kinds of data. A long tradition from Pythagoras to Galileo maintains that numbers and mathematics are the language of Nature. In the last century Lord Kelvin, speaking for the scientists, and Bentham, for the utilitarians, stressed the importance of quantification. Numerical and statistical analyses have served us well in certain areas, but it is not evident that every important aspect of our activity can be satisfactorily coded and handled by programmable procedures.

Work on artificial-intelligence is raising severe problems in the processing of non-numerical data. How, for instance, should we handle probability? Mathematics treats this as a matter of arithmetic, but our own probability judgements are qualitative and intuitive. Again, will AI be confined to expert systems and industrial robots? Or, will it be capable of taking the initiative, making informed evaluations, reconciling contradictory information, operating in natural languages and interpreting the information stores in databanks? I believe that reality will be less dramatic, and that statement to be a candidate for an anthology of purple prose, for which writings about IT could provide much material.

The distinguishing marks of intelligent behaviour in our friends certainly include creativity and the ability to learn. Some have proposed to simulate these by injecting a dash of randomness whenever an AI program reaches a key branching point: that was the technique attributed by Dean Swift to the foolish philosophers of Laputa. It is as easy to generate new patterns as it is to generate new theorems in mathematics; what is difficult but crucial is to be able to recognize that small fraction of them that is significant and will be fruitful.

When discussing IT it has become obligatory to look ahead, but we should do so with humility, for no one foresaw the microcomputer explosion. The near future will hold more of the same, as hardware becomes faster, smaller, cheaper and more reliable. Over the next decade the principal developments will be in storage devices and in telecommunications. Vast amounts of time and money will be expended on linking together computer systems using different designs of hardware. This 'networking' will generate its own problems. The most obdurate will be the interworking of diverse software, for programming shows little sign of rising above the craft level, although the growing use of packages will move us towards a standardization *de facto*. International agreement will have to be reached on effective 'protocols', i.e. on procedures for setting-up and clearing-down connections, for the validation and protection of data in transit, and for the exchange of data between programs.

In the longer term, we may be sure that new materials, new techniques and even new principles of hardware and software design will emerge. The electronic circuits on silicon chips are already microscopically small, but each contains millions of atoms. Some research is exploring the possible use of single molecules for storing and switching digital pulses. That approach offers increased capacity for data storage, and the dramatic reduction in size might allow the very much slower pace of molecular events to be offset by operating many thousands of units in parallel.

The development of AI will be pressed ahead with, for too much money has been invested, too many personal and institutional reputations are at stake, to do otherwise. Most of this work will be directed at specific expert systems rather than any attempt at a general simulation of human intelligence. No doubt we shall learn how to construct ever-more effective instruments and ever-more complicated weapons, and we must hope that we learn also how to use them wisely, and not just because they are there. However, I see no reason to fear that we have already stepped on to a slippery slope that will carry us willy-nilly to that domination by artificially intelligent machinery which is portrayed in Hans Alfvén's blackly comic vision of the future[3].

As we expand our IT systems and tie them together in more intricate ways the lack of a sound theoretical base must become a matter of increasing concern. What is now taught as 'computer science' or 'information science' in universities and polytechnics seems to me to be a somewhat eclectic ragbag – a toolkit rather than an intellectual discipline. In 1977, Christopher Strachey defined it as: 'A fashionable, interesting, difficult, and perhaps useful activity' [63]. It still is. We are still very vague about the concept of 'information', and too many workers succumb to the musky charms of technique, rather than the more austere beauty of theory. Lacking an adequate theoretical base I fear that our IT systems will continue to snowball by accretion, change by *ad hoc* patching, and metamorphose unchecked until the details of their design and operation are fully understood by no one.

Three forces drive the development of IT. The enthusiasm of its experts, the hope of future profits, and the fear of war. None of these is likely to support the study of its human and social consequences. IT's technologists, like all others, maintain that they are innocent toolmakers. Yet someone can pick up a harmless hammer and hit me on the head, and hit me harder with a heavier hammer. IT is by far the most powerful tool that men and women have ever been offered, and its increasing power may well tempt the ambitious or the ill-intentioned to use it to manipulate the rest of us to their advantage. Only a Panglossian fool would expect IT to raise moral standards. It is the people we have to watch, not the machines.

3

This business of information

The age of information

It would be boring indeed to detail the innumerable ways in which information has become important to economic activity and social cohesion. We have all been told so many times. If information really does perform so vital a function it must be very different from the disposable stuff which pours over us in an unending mish-mash of news, views and abuse. Facts, speculations and persuasion are smoothly blended – I almost wrote 'blanded' – as the trite, the trivial and the titillating are fleetingly presented as having as much claim on our attention as more important matters. We have no control over the flow, and no way of answering back. We are, of course, still allowed to turn it off, but like amputation that is a remedy of the last resort.

Perhaps the development of IT will let us select, question and compare. It is necessary to write 'perhaps' because IT merely enables, it does not compel and cannot guarantee. Strong commercial and political interests will continue to fish for our attention and strive to steer our responses. This they would be able to do all the more insidiously were we to permit our use of IT to persuade us that we were now in full control. What can come out of an IT system depends on what goes into it, and I see no rush to abandon control over the primary sources.

Few ages can have talked so much about information as our's does: certainly none has devoted so much time and effort to its collection, transport and application. History divides itself into chapters only for historians, but future economic histories of our time seem likely to contain a chapter headed 'The age of information', which will describe how, towards the end of the twentieth century, information became the principal commodity of the industrialized nations of the Western world. Yet, although information is bought and sold, it is valued as a means rather than as a product desirable in and for itself. It is, moreover, a somewhat disconcerting commodity, for it is hard to tell the false from the true.

An alternative historical analysis examines the development of techniques for recording and exchanging information. Presumably these began when explicit warnings and commands replaced grunts and gestures, and languages emerged to improve the cohesion and so the survival of the first talkative human groups. Oral tradition could then replace the slow, fumbling and uncontrollable processes of biological evolution by the self-directed transmission of knowledge from generation to generation. Writing developed first to serve the needs of commerce. It spread to less earthy activities as the scribes replaced the bards, in an early example of 'structural unemployment' arising from an advance in information technology. The scribes were themselves displaced when Gutenberg's printing press introduced our first mass-produced products. Electronic techniques are now carrying us into the next – but surely not the last – stage of development. Evidently, information technologies have long played a major part in our social development.

It is customary to demonstrate our obsession with information by reference to the growth in scientific publications. The first two scientific journals appeared around the middle of the seventeenth century; a century later there were 10; by 1850 the number had risen to about 1000, and it is thought to exceed 50 000 today[58]. The invention of the printing press provided the means but cannot be the sole cause of this rapid growth. And yet, the development of worldwide telecommunications also was followed by an explosive growth of news services: our appetite for information is insatiable. Did printing, and now IT, just happen to respond to a latent need? Or was it, rather, that enterprising suppliers perceived and exploited potential markets? Even so, they must have built on some need, or at least on our idle curiosity, although most of us are now bombarded with more information than we can absorb, and much of it is either banal or irrelevant, or both.

Data reduction

As a species we have presumably evolved to handle the input of information of the kind and at the rate which our ancestors acquired through their unaided senses as they walked or ran about the natural world. What we need, indeed what we perceive, is still closely related to what serves our survival. Our senses are now extended by instruments and by telecommunications, and data are collected and fed to us by thousands of men and women all over our planet, and by machines beyond it. Those in the information business naturally assume that if some information is good then more information will be better: but we all know that is not true. Could IT provide the filter that will save us from the flood? To attempt to answer that question we need to consider what information is, and how we use it.

Computers are often said to produce information by processing data. The word 'data' derives from a Latin root which suggests that it means 'the givens', as if data emerged spontaneously, untouched by human hands or minds. Plain men have been heard to demand loudly and fearlessly that the facts should be allowed to speak for themselves, or to assert that they have already done so; but facts are dumb brutes, and we cannot know what they tell us until we know how they were obtained and why. Facts simply do not fall unbidden on our heads, like Newton's apple: we go out and gather them with some particular purpose in mind. Any set of facts embalms its original collector's view of what was significant for whatever purpose she or he had in mind at the time. Data acquisition is an active, interventionist, process and one which necessarily selects and interprets certain aspects of the flux of events and ignores others. Even at the basic sensory level our data have been pre-selected, for there can be no doubt that we see, hear, smell, taste and feel what conduced to the survival of our remote ancestors; those among them who attended to the wrong data did not survive to breed.

Our eyes, for example, do not simply report spot-by-spot the elementary units of light and colour imaged on our retinas. There are about one hundred times as many light-sensitive cells in those retinas as there are fibres in our optic nerves. The raw optical data are processed without our knowledge or consent, and are greatly reduced in volume before they pass on to the brain. This reduction is no arbitrary procedure, the processing that takes place in nerve cells behind the retina detects patterns of illumination corresponding to moving vertical edges, and other visual features that have been important to human survival. Normally, this presents no difficulty, but in unusual situations the processing is inappropriate and we experience optical illusions.

In an IT system also, a designer in search of economy may well reduce the communications load, and relieve the central computers of routine chores, by arranging for some preliminary data reduction to take place in the remote terminals where the raw input arises. The availability of cheap and reliable microprocessors has increased the attractiveness of that option. It, too, causes no difficulty so long as the system is used for the purpose originally specified to its designer. However, as time passes, modifications will be made to suit changed circumstances, and the system will be extended and linked to other systems to serve new uses not foreseen in its original design. My fear is that its new users may then be unaware that the input data have been preprocessed. The risk may be small but it ought to be assessed explicitly, for if the preliminary processing is inappropriate the result could be the IT equivalent of optical illusions.

Of course, risks of that kind are not confined to IT systems, they are present whenever and however data collected for one purpose are used for another. Economic and social analyses are often based on the use of time-series of data collected over many years, and such series need to be interpreted with great care. To take just one example from many in Morgenstern's splendid book[49], the suicide rate in the USA rose abruptly when it ceased to be a crime, for doctors were then prepared to report it as the cause of death. That example illustrates another point. The lower tiers of any organization – business or government department – are accustomed to 'massage' the facts as they pass upwards in order to insulate their masters from uncomfortable revelations. A new IT system, designed by hawkish young specialists who are stronger on the theory of management than on the actualities of its practice, may hamper this 'tempering of the wind' for a while; but we may be reasonably confident that those who have to work with the system will eventually learn how to work it. The lessons are: first, that facts are never just bare facts, they are 'facts for' some purpose; second, we must seek to understand that purpose and know exactly why and how data were collected before we attempt to use them.

Numerical data

An isolated fact is rarely useful, and it is not until facts are organized on some basis of understanding that they become 'knowledge'. The sciences are possibly our most impressive body of knowledge, and most of the facts on which they rest are numerical – the results of measurements. In the nineteenth century, Lord Kelvin said forcefully that unless our knowledge was numerical it was of a 'meagre and unsatisfactory kind'. His warning would not have been necessary today for we have moved to the opposite pole and risk falling into 'numerolatry', the idolatrous worship of numbers[33]. Numbers are certainly seductive, for when someone replies '14.87%' we feel that she really does know what she is talking about. We tend to pay far too much respect to foolish figures, measuring everything that it is easy to measure and dressing up what we cannot measure in arbitrary numerical values.

In the West, the cry for literacy has been replaced by that for numeracy, as we shift our allegiance from Lord Byron to his daughter, Ada. Without doubt the mandarins have had a long innings, but replacing them with calculating technocrats may not be an unqualified improvement. It is not true that the only things that count are those that can be counted. A trained palate and a sensitive nose are arguably the best, and certainly the most pleasant, way of dealing with the uncoded data that emerge from a good claret. Any clever fool can generate a string of numbers, and many do: interpretation is all, and requires two much rarer talents, wisdom and insight. The development of IT is not, of course, the sole reason for our fascination with figures. In the eighteenth century, Edmund Burke was lamenting that the Age of Chivalry had been succeeded by 'that of sophisters, economists and calculators'.[15]. Sophisters was a shrewd thrust, for the sophists were notorious for meretricious reasoning, and some of our own uses of numerical data could fall under the same condemnation.

Like it or not, numerical data do dominate many applications of IT, and it is important to distinguish clearly between three attributes that are frequently confused. They are accuracy, precision and significance. Thus, the gross national product (GNP) of a nation is a matter for continual comment, and has become a symbol of economic virility. Commonly quoted to a precision of $\pm\,0.1\%$, it is indeed a better class of national statistics, for it can be measured to an accuracy of $\pm\,3\%$. For a movement in GNP to be significant, indeed to be able to say whether it went up or down, its change needs to exceed the bounds of its error range – it must be more than $\pm\,3\%$. Yet journalists report, economists agonize, and politicians pontificate about alleged movements of fractions of 1%. Worse still, they propose remedies to correct changes that no one can truly discern. Fortunately, it is rare for any of their remedies to be put into practice, nor is any of them certainly known to have much effect. Revised figures for GNP appear after a year or two when the facts are better known, and the published corrections amount to 1% or 2% either way for the more reliable national series, such as those of the UK or the USA.[49].

The monthly balance-of-payment figures are another closely watched statistic, but one whose fluctuations depend fortuitously on whether some particularly large bill was paid before or after the end of the month in question. And, in Britain adverse import figures are usually offset by large, and suspiciously round-figure, estimates of invisible earnings from financial services. Many economic and social statistics are like those meaningless medals which military politicians use to cover their chests and their pretensions. In Devon, we call such people 'Admirals on a winkle barge', and they and their statistics should be no more than 'A source of innocent merriment'[28]. Unfortunately, both have acquired the power to mislead and misdirect.

In summary, precision is how many decimal digits are used to express a numerical fact; accuracy is how many of them are correct; and significance is how many of them are important. I can recommend the regular use of three simple rules when faced with numerical data.

– For uncertain accuracy: challenge any figure that is not accompanied by an estimate of its error range; data are as subject to error as a dog is to fleas; view with caution any analysis which does not take data errors into account, few do.

– For inflated precision: examine the extreme right-hand digit and consider what you would feel bound to do were it to change by ± 3; if nothing, delete it and replace by zero; repeat this procedure moving to the left until some action or change of opinion is indicated. (This remedy is highly effective for treating the inflamed precision of stock exchange indices; thus, the Nikkei-Dow is quoted to two decimal places, but can change by 100 units overnight.)

– For false prestige: reflect that figures issued by large organizations, governments especially, are statistical sermons whose function is to exhort rather than to inform.

Bits and bytes

When considering the design and operation of IT systems we need some way of measuring the amount of information being handled. Claude Shannon developed such a measure in the context of telecommunications, and it has been widely applied to computing also. He considered information in its most basic telegraphic form, as a sequence of on–off pulses of electric current flowing through a wire. Each such pulse can be used to convey one binary digit, where, say, current-off stands for 0 and current-on stands for 1.

Before continuing, it may be useful to say a little about binary. In everyday life we unhesitatingly count and calculate with the familiar decimal digits 0,1,2. . .9 without pausing to think that we do so only because we happen to have 10 fingers. Decimal numbers are not particularly convenient for arithmetic and other number systems have been used in the past. The design and manufacture of IT hardware becomes simpler if its electronic circuits have to discriminate only between current and no current, rather than between electric currents of 10 different strengths. So, it is preferable to represent numbers in a way that requires only the two kinds of digit, 0 and 1.

When numbers are expressed in that 'binary notation' the successive digits stand for units, twos, fours, eights, and so on, instead of units, tens, hundreds, thousands. . . , as in decimal. For instance, binary 1011 represents one unit, plus one two, no four and one eight, namely 1+2+0+8, written as 11 in decimal. Pen and pencil arithmetic is just as easy in binary as in decimal but more tedious because more digits have to be written down, and many more carries made from one column to the next. An introductory chapter on binary used to be obligatory in all books on computers, but it is of concern here only as a background to Shannon's measure of information. The use of binary inside IT systems presents no difficulty to their users, for the inputs and outputs are automatically, inconspicuously and rapidly converted to and from binary by special-purpose hardware.

The basic unit of information, Shannon style, is one binary digit (0 or 1), invariably abbreviated to one 'bit'; it is just fortuitous that the English word bit also means a small piece. A group of four bits can represent any number from binary 0000 = 0 to binary 1111 = 15, and such a group is commonly used for the decimal digits. IBM introduced the name 'byte' for a group of eight bits which its computers handled as a unit and, like so many of IBM's standards, that term has been universally adopted. One byte can represent any of 256 different 'characters', which is amply sufficient to cover the Roman alphabet in upper and lower case, plus punctuation marks, the decimal numerals and some symbols. When describing the performance of IT systems the larger units 'kilobytes' (kB) and 'megabytes' (MB) more conveniently specify the information storage capacity, and in the forms kB/s and MB/s the rates of transmission over data links. Strictly speaking, k means the 'binary thousand' 1024, and M means the 'binary million' 1 048 576; but it is rarely necessary to apply those small corrections. Kilobytes and megabytes feature prominently in advertising material, for the publicity issued by IT system suppliers understandably focuses on things that are easy to measure and have a whiff of technical wizardry, rather than on those of greater importance to users – just as car advertising makes much of maximum speeds that few drivers will ever attempt to attain. The danger is that the designers of commercial systems may be deflected into chasing after meaningless performance figures to win a transient marketing advantage.

Shannon's measure of information was developed by a communications engineer for use by communications engineers. Telecommunication companies are in the transportation business; known as 'common carriers', their job is to deliver customers' messages to distant points. They tend to assume that those messages do in fact convey information, but that is none of their business. Shannon's measure attributes no more bits to one of Shakespeare's sonnets than to an equal number of randomly chosen letters. Furniture removers measure the Venus de Milo in kilograms, and Picassos by the square metre; and communication engineers are concerned professionally only with the number of bits they are asked to convey, and not with their meaning or significance. If the customer will pay, they will carry anything. Indeed, as we shall see when we discuss the question of privacy, their customers are anxious that the common carriers should not take too much interest in the contents of the messages they convey.

Shannon's bits, therefore, have their limitations. They take no account of many attributes of importance to the users of information. It lies outside our present purpose to attempt to list all of these, but accuracy, precision and relevance are obviously desirable in every application; and timeliness, completeness and exclusiveness are important to business users. Again, information only becomes so when it *in*-forms, that is changes the form of someone's thoughts. Hence, two other qualities are specific to each individual recipient. The first is novelty; telling me what I already know conveys no information. The second is connectivity; to be useful to me, information must link in at the right level with what I already know and be consistent with it.

It is in terms of qualities like these that the computers in IT systems can be said to convert data into information. No communication link and no computer can increase the amount of information *à la mode de* Shannon which is carried by a data message. At best, we can hope that they will not decrease it unacceptably by introducing electrical noise and interference, or by misbehaving, or by processing it under the control of an inaccurate, incomplete or inappropriate program. However, a computer can greatly enhance the value of its input data by selection, combination with other data previously entered and stored, and by correlation analyses. But that increase in value cannot be measured in bits or bytes, and it varies from user to user.

An important class of information consists not of data but of instructions – instructions in computer programs, and orders to coordinate the actions of men and women. Our understanding of the consequences that can develop from obeying a given set of instructions is feeble. We find it virtually impossible to predict the remoter consequences of applying quite elementary rules. This is easily illustrated by using a simple program to generate patterns on a video screen. The results may be predictable in principle, but can be quite unexpected[55]. We urgently need more research into this aspect of information theory, but unfortunately research has to wait for insight and that cannot be conjured up even by liberal applications of money.

Money has its principal part to play in the much more costly stages of development and design which follow success in research (the D of R&D), and it is attracted to those activities by the prospects of short-term gains and the assurance of achieving results. Research is a long-term speculation. Most current work on advanced IT systems is carried out under development projects funded by governments to meet what they perceive to be their defence requirements. And, when the universities are underfunded, their computer scientists tend to be deflected from research into short-term development and design, especially when their paymasters cry for greater 'relevance'. That diversion could have seriously adverse consequences in the longer term. I am convinced that, say, 10% of the money provided for any development project should be made available to support unspecified basic research in the same subject area. Otherwise information science may become indistinguishable from computing practice, and fail to establish the fundamental principles sorely needed by those who are busily erecting ever-more elaborate structures on shallow foundations. Outside of its original application to computation, we have a disturbingly weak understanding of the theoretical base of an activity which absorbs so much time and money, and which pervades so many aspects of our lives. Success in numerical computation does not entail, and certainly cannot guarantee, success in applications more closely related to the fuzzy everyday world inhabited by men and women. We shall return to this point when discussing safety and security in Chapter 7.

Computer modelling

Where our understanding is weak, we fall back on the method of modelling [19,24]. Economists, for example, have set themselves the fearsomely difficult task of analysing one aspect of the behaviour of complex social systems. Their principal problems are to decide which economic quantities they should include and which to treat as exogenous, and then to specify with sufficient precision the relationships they believe to hold between them. That stage depends above all else on the perceptive formulation of hypotheses, and IT can offer little help in that exercise of the creative imagination. Not every hypothesis proposes causal mechanisms, for it is very much easier to postulate mathematical relationships which merely describe. The set of equations, or inequalities, used to express the behaviour of some system constitutes a 'mathematical model' of it.

When the activities are simple and the equations are few, the only tools required are a pencil and paper. More realistic models deploy many variables and large sets of equations, and are most conveniently handled by programming a computer to perform the corresponding calculations. Indeed, it would often be quite impracticable to do anything else. The computer has then been set up to simulate the operation of the system, and the model has become a 'computer model', meaning, of course, one driven by a computer and not one modelling the action of a computer. Our ability to cope with models of great complexity in this way can tempt the unwary into piling on *ad hoc* features in search of greater realism. We have all seen rococco models in which elaboration has taken over from insight. Computers never absolve us from the need to think.

Nevertheless, computer models are powerful tools of analysis that offer a number of advantages.

- They can cope with as many variables and relationships as any reasonable analyst is likely to require, and many more simultaneous interactions than could ever be handled in words alone.
- They can employ non-linear, bounded, threshold, delayed, feedback, probabilistic and other awkward relationships which are difficult or impossible to handle by the methods of formal analysis.
- They can be quickly and easily processed repeatedly in order to reveal how sensitive are the results to variations in the input data or in the assumed relationships between variables, which allows an economist, say, to experiment with a surrogate system to test and develop his or her ideas.
- As compared with purely verbal description and argument, the construction of a model forces us to state our theses and assumptions precisely and unambiguously.

Nevertheless, even the most refined model is a gross simplification of reality, and we can never be certain that every important factor has been included and given its proper weight. Unfortunately, it is not possible to check a model by retrodiction, for either the appropriate historical data will not exist, or they will have been used in devising the model itself. There is also the danger that a model which at first enlarges our understanding may come to contract it by rejecting data that do not conform. Theoreticians find models irresistible, but their combination of complexity with mathematics can confuse or repel the less academically minded, which reduces their explanatory value for managers and administrators.

Except for 'black-box' models which merely describe the overall relationships, with no hypothesis about what goes on inside the box, we hope that a successful model does in fact represent the factors operating in the real world. So far as that is so, the model will simulate the system's dynamic behaviour as well as its static equilibrium states. Dynamic behaviour is of very great importance in human systems, for large transient disturbances often accompany changes from one state to another and can be more troublesome than either the initial or the final states themselves. Thus, the introduction of a new technology is said to cause temporary 'structural unemployment' as workers move out of newly obsolete, and await entry into newly created, jobs. It is important to establish whether a given model is just a black box that happens to fit recent data and conditions. We noted earlier the risks of attributing more exactitude and relevance to the output of an IT system than its data or its programs can justify.

Information-rich, information-poor

Optimists predict that the spread of IT systems will make valuable information and computing facilities universally available. That, they argue, will be an unadulterated public good for it will increase the ability of the ordinary man and woman to understand, to influence and to challenge the actions and policies of governments and other large corporations that bear upon their lives. But will it really be like that?

The computing cliché GIGO (Garbage in, garbage out) serves to remind us that IT systems are not automated alchemists; they cannot transmute dross into gold. No matter how subtle the processing, the information we can extract depends critically on the nature and quality of the input data. They who control those inputs control all possible outputs. We can confidently predict that vast numbers of Shannon's megabytes will slosh about inside our IT systems, but to what extent will they represent relevant, unambiguous, accurate and complete information? IT systems can shift immense amounts of data, but unless their programming is accurate and appropriate they will merely sweep it up into tidy, but irrelevant, heaps. We hear cries for more open government, usually from opposition parties before they win elections. And there are cries for companies to disclose more business information, more often from trade unions than from ordinary shareholders dozing over their dividends. These appeals could be met by discharging periodic floods of facts, with the intention of choking the cat with cream, but the cream will have been prudently pasteurized – in the wider public interest, of course.

Attempts are being made to set standards for 'open systems interconnection' (OSI), which will allow different IT systems to be connected together. One result could be a public information service offering access to an international range of 'databanks', computer stores acting as reference libraries. Viewdata systems are a primitive form of such a service. Who would derive most benefit? Not the poor, because access to remote databanks, and the purchase or hire of the software for mathematical modelling or statistical analysis, cannot be cheap, and are most unlikely to be provided free of charge. Not the undereducated either, for data derive their value by slotting into what we already know. Esoteric new biochemical facts, however important and accurate, mean nothing to me for I know no biochemistry. IT will help most those members of society who least need its help, namely, the highly educated, the well-informed, the well-off and the politically active.

Technologically minded utopians predict that IT will strengthen the links that bind individuals into a society. It seems possible that it will be socially divisive, widening the gap between the 'information-rich' and the 'information-poor'. It is worrying that those categories correlate with economic riches and poverty. Those who will benefit most from the availability of IT systems also include pressure groups of various kinds, for they are usually spear-headed by active members of the literate, numerate and highly articulate middle class. Concerned with single issues, such as the conservation of the environment, the implications of reinforcing their political muscle are considered in Chapter 8. So also are the effects that our use of IT may have on enlarging the rift between the economically underprivileged and information-poor nations of the Third World and those of the industrially advanced and information-rich Western 'First World'.

Technologists are apt to say, defensively, that their methods and their machines are neutral, and are available to serve good purposes as well as ill. They add that responsibility for human and social damage must therefore rest with those who through ignorance, clumsiness or sheer malevolence misuse the splendid instruments they have provided. Fire can roast an ox or burn a heretic. Ordinary women and men rarely find that argument convincing. They have a gut feeling that just as it would be unwise to place the latest design of kitchen knife in the hands of a baby, so it might be better to withhold some of the sharper tools that technologists now so naively provide – wagging their tails and obviously expecting a biscuit and a pat on the head as they do so. This matter is taken up in Chapter 8.

Postscript

It was Bergson who suggested that our brains evolved not so much to capture information as to protect us from being overwhelmed by the flood of data streaming in from our senses. In our more conscious phases of thought, we accept information when it fits our working hypothesis – the model of whatever we happen to be attending to – and we reject it when it does not. Facts cannot live in a vacuum, their existence and their very nature depend on our reason for collecting them, and our interpretation of them is strongly influenced by the society and culture in which we live[9].

Unemployment statistics, for example, are published as cold facts, and chilling figures they undoubtedly are. Their value, however, depends on the precise meaning attached to 'unemployment' and government and opposition squabble as much about its definition as about the more vital question of its cure. IT systems can collect and present whatever facts we require, and do so rapidly and accurately, but they cannot reconcile differences of definition, nor establish who, if anyone, is right.

Because data are collected for some particular purpose, and are not absolute, I wonder how far it will prove to be useful to set up non-specific stores of information, omnipurpose databanks. In many matters my facts are not likely to be your facts, and those available from databanks will be the ones acceptable to whoever deposited them. Those criticisms apply also to an encyclopaedia or a reference library. The better encyclopaedias list their contributors, which enables us to weigh their authority and recall their prejudices. The professional staff of reference libraries are trained to direct enquirers to the sources that best meet their needs. IT services will have to deploy equivalent ways of authenticating the information they purvey. IT provides a versatile, and now indispensable, instrument of enlightenment, but we must beware of allowing the glitter of hi-tech to dazzle us into believing everything that someone has programmed our systems to select and display on their video screens.

IT is not being developed to meet any crying need of ordinary men and women for information, we have a surfeit of that already. We ourselves, and the institutions of our societies, have evolved for survival in an environment where information was scarce and its distribution far from uniform. As yet more information becomes ever more widely available, there will be severe problems of adaptation, with casualties among those who fail to do so. In commerce, men and women have succeeded by acquiring earlier, fuller and more accurate information than their competitors. If the promise of comprehensive and universally available economic and commercial information were to be realized, then it would revive that 'market with perfect information' which used to grace the early pages of economic textbooks.

In public affairs, a ready access to the past promises of aspiring politicians, and to analyses of what they subsequently did to implement them, would introduce an interesting constraint into electioneering. In professional work, the development of improved expert systems could do for the run-of-the-mill practitioner what television and its stars have done to reduce the acceptability of amateur performers. The professional institutions would then be forced to adapt to a declining membership, and to rethink both their training requirements and their role in society. Television's worldwide news services bring vivid images of distant disasters into our homes as they are occurring, and those who live in large cities may be better informed about antipodean strangers than about their neighbours. In these and many other ways IT is accelerating the pace of social change.

IT systems will continue to develop in size and in richness of interconnection, until, perhaps, they reach the limit which Lord Bowden foresaw when he wrote of the early computers that 'it took the united efforts of the staff to keep them on the verge of operation'[12]. It may be that IT systems are increasing rapidly in the complexity of hardware, and even more of interconnection and of software, towards that Bowden Limit at which they will just not work long enough between crashes to establish that they are doing what we want them to do. Depending on the importance of their application, the social consequences of that situation could be serious indeed, and far from obvious in advance.

We urgently need more research into the theory of information systems, and into the ways we make use of information. Because that is a long-term undertaking with no guarantee of early profits, and because inspiration cannot be forced by considerations of 'relevance', it is work which can be carried out only in the universities. I am not persuaded that their currently fashionable obsession with AI is an adequate substitute, for most of that activity is directed towards practical outcomes and urgent timetables – both industrial and military. When in hot pursuit of economies, boards of directors and governments are always tempted to cut pure research, for that is easy to do and has no immediately adverse effect. It is the same with vitamins; in each case the deficiency reveals itself in long-term weaknesses which may not then be quickly corrected.

4

Economics and IT

The effect of IT on employment requires a chapter of its own (see Chapter 5). Here, we consider some other economic consequences which bear on the formulation of policies by governments and large corporations whose actions impinge on us at many points.

The dismal science

We are bombarded with interpretations of events by amateur and professional economists who tend to agree in disliking current policies, although their reasons differ as widely as the remedies they propose. Economists have not yet formulated a common body of theory, and instead of a science we have a hubbub of competing schools. Two reasons contribute to this sorry state of affairs: the frailty of economic data, and the impossibility of testing hypotheses by controlled experiments on real societies.

Refined statistical techniques – their use being often a sign of theoretical weakness – can sometimes be used to reduce the consequences of input error. IT may be able to help by gathering data where they arise, as when a cash register records item-by-item purchases as they are made. This 'data capture at source' will certainly increase the volume of raw material, but its quality will improve only if the data are the right ones, and representative of their kind, for they can never be complete.

Absence of theory is more troublesome, for not even a tonne of computation can make up for the lack of a gram of insight. We may hope that computer modelling will offer some help by enabling economists to test alternative models and eliminate the unfit. Models can also change public perceptions, as did the now abandoned one behind the Club of Rome's scary report on *The Limits to Growth* [24, 44, 45]. But, even when a model does produce results that correspond well enough with recent events we have to accept that social values, goals and priorities change continually. Technological changes also will produce major deviations, for genuine novelty is notoriously unpredictable, but can be dramatic in effect (Fig. 1). Again, exports are a major factor but are exceptionally difficult to forecast, for they depend on actions which foreign customers will take in their own interests. Moreover, to the extent that a model influences the thinking of businessmen or the decisions of politicians its results feed back to change the future it was designed to predict.

The more closely a government controls its economy and manages social affairs the more predictable the future should be. It would be fanciful, however, to deduce the converse proposition and conclude that by encouraging the use of automatic data capture and computer models IT will promote the evolution of a planned economy. Nevertheless, the use of quantitative methods is undoubtedly congenial to managerially minded politicians, and we need to remain alert and ready to resist developments that ignore humane objectives and seek only to

Fig. 1. Who, extrapolating the caterpillar, would predict the butterfly?

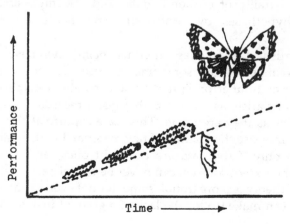

maximize the measurable. The principal value of computer models is to ensure that the plans we make separately for different economic sectors are mutually consistent, and form a coherent whole. The danger is that the speed and apparent precision of modelling may tempt us to take instant decisions about economic policy, rather than allow time for snags to be foreseen, and objections to emerge.

It was not its theoretical weakness that led Carlyle [16] to describe political economy as 'The dismal science', although a comparison of the progress made since the last century in physical science with that achieved in economics does warrant that epithet. Galileo was once moved to admiration that men could so far trust their reasoning as 'to commit such a rape on their senses' by believing that the Earth moved around the sun, despite abundant everyday evidence to the contrary. We do not need to treat our common sense quite so roughly when it happens to challenge economic results issuing from a computer analysis for 'economic knowledge, though not neglibible, is so extremely imperfect. . . . There are few economic "laws" which can be regarded as at all firmly based'[30]. Galbraith has been equally scathing[26].

Automation

The introduction of automation into offices and factories has major consequences for the whole of industry and commerce. The subject is too large to be handled in a few pages, but it is outlined below to indicate why it attracts so much anxious discussion.

The first applications of computers to office work were to payroll, stock control, job costing and other humdrum activities of accountants. That those functions were so easily taken over showed not that computers were clever enough to compete with clerks, but only that this was rule-bound, mechanical work which men and women need no longer perform, and which never had required human intelligence. It was soon apparent that computers could also provide support for managers by improving the collection and analysis of business data. Moreover, when combined with electronic communications within the office, they offered direct access to a central pool of information (a common database) whose use, it was hoped, would increase the effectiveness of business decisions. All this provided a fertile field for management consultancy; but experience has shown that the amount a firm spends on office automation is not at all closely correlated with the effectiveness of its managers[64].

IT systems are not fussy about the value of the information they handle, and much office work serves no useful purpose – or does so no longer. It was easy but inept to take over existing office activities just as they were; in fact, a stringent review of all data and every procedure is essential before any attempt is made at automation. The offices of large organizations tend to swell until they reach a critical mass at which they divide into specialist branches, and at this point interbranch communications rise sharply and swamp those with the real world outside. In such cases, it is futile to substitute electronics for paper for, although junk electronic mail travels faster and costs more, it can claim no other advantage. Moreover, its video displays are endurable, and may even be exciting, for brief messages, but they are tedious and visually tiring for longer memoranda.

Properly used, however, IT can result in more effective management by releasing managers from their cosy housekeeping exchanges with colleagues, and enabling them to move from solving internal problems to seeking external opportunities. In this way they return to close contact with their real business of producing goods and providing services for actual customers. In Britain, the attitude of senior managers to IT has been ambivalent. On the one hand, they feel the need, most acutely just before a meeting of shareholders, to demonstrate their active concern to reduce office costs. On the other hand, their fear and dislike of technology has led them to cultivate an attitude of lofty ignorance, and to leave the design of office systems to IT specialists on the principle of not keeping a dog and barking oneself. There is then a risk that your dog may bark to please herself or, if male, to impress other dogs. The inclination and training of IT specialists lead them to see the management of a business as a network of information channels which intersect at nodal points, where managers sit and consistently apply rational decision rules. Neither offices nor managers are like that; nor are the important channels at all like those portrayed on the – always obsolete – organization chart. These inconvenient circumstances are shrugged-off by system designers as aberrations that their work will correct. That mistaken conception has held back the expected benefits of the higher office automation, and its principal effects have been confined to the lower levels of work in the large clerical factories of banking, insurance and government departments. We should welcome what IT has done in those places to deliver men and women from grinding, subhuman routine. Some of those liberated, however, see it rather as a loss of employment opportunities, and that is the subject of the next chapter.

For the first attempts to automate office work, only large computers were available and these are likely to continue to be used to manage the larger files – the central databanks – of corporate headquarters. Much of the processing has been devolved to microcomputers operated by individual office workers. Even mass-production tasks, once centralized, have been dispersed. For example, meter readers carry portable computers into customers' premises not only to record their consumption of electricity but also to calculate and print their bills on the spot. Instead of typewriters, secretaries use microprocessors disguised as word-processors which save them much time and untold frustration when faced with the nth redraft of a memorandum. They are invaluable also for churning out implausibly 'personalized' versions of standard documents and circular letters.

Combined with a laser printer, a word-processor can generate printed text and diagrams of impressively high quality. This has been hailed as the launch of 'desk-top publishing' which will compete seriously with jobbing printers. However, considerable skill is required to produce an attractive layout, and to select and combine different type-faces. It seems rather more likely that, once the novelty has worn off, publishing services will again be bought in from the professionals; they may well themselves use word processors and laser printers, but will do so more effectively. The implications of IT for the printer's trade, in the newspaper industry particularly, are considered in the next chapter.

Factory automation conjures up visions of robotic production lines, but although these make good television commercials they have not yet advanced very far. We are still at a primitive stage in which our robots are little more than tightly programmed machines that position materials and components at automatic work-stations and move partially finished products on from station to station. IT is being used more adventurously in industrial design offices where its visual display techniques enable designers to examine and manipulate three-dimensional images of their creations. IT helps also with the routine tasks of a drawing office, above all with the tedious and error-prone chore of ensuring that modifications to some common component are carried into the drawings and specifications of every product in which it happens to have been used. IT links designers closely to the shop floor. The acronym CAD (computer-aided design) names a system in which the design is expressed as a computer output that can be used directly to control machine tools. The use of these numerically controlled tools not only saves time and labour it also reduces the amount of scrap material and the number of rejects. CAD combines readily with CAM (computer-aided manufacture), a suite of programs which coordinates the production process, ensuring that adequate – but not excessive – supplies of raw materials are available in stock, and that expensive tools do not stand idle.

These uses of IT should reduce costs, but equally importantly they will combine uniformity of product with fewer manufacturing faults, and by way of 'customized mass production' they enable a manufacturer to offer a large number of variations on a single theme. One popular model of car is advertised as being available to customer's order in any of several billion trivial variations. Moreover, production lines using programmable machines can switch rapidly from one product to another of a broadly similar kind. This flexibility allows more sources of work to be tapped to keep the machines fully employed. Long runs are no longer necessary to achieve low costs. It is possible, for instance, to make valves for the engines of many different models of car in small batches on demand, and thus avoid the need to keep large stocks. But that flexibility is the result of human choices between rigidly pre-programmed alternatives; it is not an automatic response to unforeseen circumstances.

Another industrial use of IT is to relieve human operators of inherently dirty, noisy or dangerous tasks. Chemical plants, oil refineries, steel rolling-mills, the production of paper and of cement, nuclear power stations and the extractive industries have all been subject to automatic control. The complexity of today's plants makes them difficult to comprehend, and operators can be slow to respond to a crisis: boredom and fatigue can lower their performance, and when key operators are absent the plant may stand idle. The prime motive for automatic control in the process industries has been cost reduction but, as a beneficial side-effect, working conditions have been greatly improved – for those who remain in work. Safety is enhanced, energy is saved and pollution has also been reduced.

As with office automation, it is regular routine work which is most readily mechanized. IT is much less successful where a production worker has to cope with unpredictable situations, or to make judgments based on insight, experience or common sense. One of the principal reasons for work on AI is its promise of increasing the adaptability and the 'expertise' of automatic control systems.

The long-term consequences of automation in offices, warehouses and factories are not easy to predict. Many of them are unplanned and unexpected side-effects which arise from the interaction of human, social and political factors outside the control, and often beyond the knowledge, of the system's designers. It would be more than usually lucky if all of them were pleasant. And yet no one deliberately sets out to produce unpleasant antisocial consequences, just as no one sets out to pollute the environment. Users of IT and the polluters are each too closely intent on their own short-term economic gains to look out for the spill-overs that trouble others.

'Smart' products and services

The use of IT, microprocessors particularly, has become essential in product design. Any new appliance or instrument that needs, or can be induced to incorporate, complex automatic controls or fancy displays will fail to match its competitors unless it can be advertised as 'intelligent'. That adjective is an obvious misnomer; the American word 'smart' is preferable, and conveys just the right hint of superficial slickness.

We hear a great deal about the movement of Western economies into a 'post-industrial' phase in which the provision of services will replace the production of goods. This may be true in general but the reverse movement has taken place in middle-class homes. The industrial revolution dried up the supply of cheap domestic servants – mainly young women from rural areas – by offering them better pay and a more impersonally subservient employment. Their services are now provided by mechanized household goods, vacuum cleaners, polishers, washing machines and so on, in which electric motors first replaced their muscles and IT is now replacing their skills.

A glance at the new products introduced over the last decade or so reveals how many of them are based on the microelectronic components (silicon chips) developed for IT. Clocks and watches, calculators and cameras, cash registers and weighing machines, typewriters, security locks, measuring instruments, smart credit cards, sophisticated toys and awesome weapons – the list lengthens daily. Every small mechanism and every automatic control is giving way to electronics. Their manufacturers benefit because they find it easier, cheaper and quicker to design and produce new features and facilities. Customers benefit from the smaller size, lower cost and greater reliability of electronic devices. Workers who once made the displaced mechanisms have little doubt about IT's economic consequences for them.

Two interrelated developments are known as 'point of sale' (POS) recording and 'electronic funds transfer' (EFT). Those who work with IT are inordinately fond of initials and acronyms: the most charitable explanation is that they are accustomed to take their information in a coded form, but it is also possible that they delight in cloaking their art in mystery. Point-of-sale recording is to be found in supermarkets where the cash registers read coded labels that indicate not only the prices but also the nature and quantity of goods purchased customer-by-customer. The advantages for sales analysis and stock control are obvious, but customers can find that once familiar items have been displaced in favour of others that are revealed to earn a higher profit per square metre of shelf space.

Purchases are paid for by inserting a plastic card into the cash register, which thereupon sends a data signal directly to the customer's bank to trigger an automatic electronic transfer of funds from his or her account. Some cards incorporate a slim microprocessor on a silicon chip. These 'smart cards' store records of the customer's current balance to guard against overspending, and can carry personal codes and other private information to identify the user and hinder their dishonest use by unauthorized persons. The use of smart cards is seductively convenient and is still optional; but they could metamorphose insidiously into personal identity cards, invaluable for a state wishing to control its citizens.

As well as the manufacture of hardware and the production of software, IT has stimulated the development of information services tailored to suit the needs of an individual customer. Known sometimes as 'value-added services', the value they add for, say, the senior management of a company is that of providing an independent source of information to check on what their own staff is telling them. They do so by expert analyses which interpret the relevance of public and other sources of information to the client's affairs. As one supplier said: 'It's not quantity our clients need, it's succinct, salient information. They want the bottom line: do I or don't I?'[(60)].

Two less-specific kinds of information service, the IT equivalents of reference libraries, offer access to large databanks of news and other general information. Some of them operate selectively in response to individual enquiries transmitted over two-way data links already installed for telephone or cable-television services: British Telecom pioneered these viewdata services with its *Prestel*. The other kind has the generic name teletext and is superimposed on broadcast television services, for example, *Oracle* and *Ceefax* in Britain. Enquiries cannot be made but viewers can 'scroll' through the whole to locate and display particular 'pages' of information.

The management of complexity

IT's computers enable us to cope with the complex and massive data handling required for the management of very large organizations; and IT's telecommunications enable tight central control to be extended worldwide. Large multinational corporations use these powers to maximize their business opportunities and to secure commercial gains which have not always coincided with the interests of their employees or remained in their host countries. Some of these giant concentrations of economic power are mere conglomerates, assembled to spread their investment risks over a diverse collection of products and services. Others have grown by developing the export of a product to the point at which profits can be increased, or tariffs evaded, by setting up factories in or near lucrative markets.

There may be political advantages also, for the host country may be glad to reduce its import bill; and the employment given to local staff is of mutual economic benefit. However, the result can be to kill off indigenous competitors, especially where there are high fixed costs which confer advantages on large-scale operation. The unremitting pressure to develop and introduce new IT products involves particularly high fixed costs and has attracted multinational operation. Fortunately, invention waits on ingenuity, and those with the largest purse have not always produced the best ideas.

Supplying a local market is not the only reason for manufacturing overseas: lower wages, financial inducements, relaxed labour laws, and more compliant workers all play their part. Multinationals have been criticized for discouraging recruitment by trade unions, for locating their factories away from countries and large cities where unions are most active, and for dividing up their operations in other ways designed to frustrate union power; and also by their implicit threat to take their work elsewhere. Conditions favouring multinationals are often to be found in the less-developed countries, but the balance of advantage to them is far from clear. On the one hand, a company may bring in advanced new technologies, and incidentally raise the levels of education and health services by its requirements for labour. On the other hand, adverse effects may follow from forcing the pace of social and economic changes foreign to the local culture. It is not yet compulsory to work for one of these companies, but as they prosper they reduce the opportunities for finding alternative work.

Central control over the manufacture of components in particular countries and their assembly in others enables a multinational corporation to locate its profits and losses where they best fit the local tax laws, by adjusting the internal transfer prices between its plants. Financial matters also are centrally planned and controlled, and international companies naturally seek to promote their own best interests; indeed their legal obligation to their shareholders requires them to do so. Pursuit of those interests can generate short-term transfers of liquid funds between countries in order to benefit from fluctuations in interest or exchange rates. These companies are not, of course, the only or even the principal organizations seeking quick and easy profits. The amounts of money can be very large, and the virtually instantaneous transfers made possible by IT can induce instability in money markets, and may run counter to the financial policies of national governments.

International finance is only one service whose sole product is information, and which, by using IT, can be located anywhere. Industrial design, corporate management, and above all the production of software, are other examples, and we could well see such services contracted-out to specialist suppliers located in low-cost countries, or in 'havens' with relaxed attitudes to taxation and to data protection.

Clearly IT is adding to the possibilities of conflict between private and public interests. The budgets of many large corporations are larger than those of the smaller nations, and their number is increasing, for as Jan Brouwer of Shell has said: 'The nation-state in most cases has already become too small a unit to provide a competitive industrial organization with an adequately large envelope'[14]. It is not that the state has become too small, the companies have become too large. World trade is becoming ever more closely interdependent, and many important economic decisions are now being taken not by governments for reasons of public policy but in board rooms, where the primary criterion is private advantage. It is the use of IT that informs those decisions and makes them effective.

Multinational corporations provide an example of what has been called 'external integration', or 'electronic data interchange' (EDI), in which a business is linked to its bankers, suppliers and principal customers by direct automatic exchanges of data between its computers and theirs. This has been slow to take off owing to the diversity of equipment and communication protocols, and to the lack of standard terms for use on invoices and other business 'documents'. Additional problems can arise when data are transmitted across national borders, for some countries apply legal restraints which limit the information that can be passed – although it is far from easy to see how they can enforce them. One possible consequence of thorough-going external integration is for a company to grow by 'vertical integration', in which it takes over the business of its suppliers and its larger customers. The resulting concentration of economic power offers private benefits, but is not necessarily a matter for public rejoicing.

Home-grown IT

Some maintain that because the use of IT has become so pervasive, a nation must have an IT industry of its own: there are six usual lines of argument. The first rests on the adverse effects on a country's balance of payments if it has to import most of its IT equipment. Undoubtedly those effects are substantial and are increasing, although they are purely national and do not affect world trade. The second argument is that the manufacture of IT products is an exceptionally efficient converter of imports into exports, for it consumes little energy and few raw materials – software production especially. Moreover, by succeeding in so technologically advanced an activity a nation boosts its 'image' and promotes the sales of its other products also.

The third argument claims that the absence of a local workforce skilled in IT would be seriously damaging to the whole economy. That we may doubt; the important skills are those of using IT, not those involved in the manufacture of its hardware, which is in any event increasingly automated. The fourth argument is that the manufacture of IT equipment is part of a general trend away from heavy industry, so that any country that fails to follow this trend will simply miss an opportunity to replace its older industries, which will inevitably decline.

The fifth argument is that a nation which relies on imported equipment will not be able to deploy the latest designs, with the result that its users will fall behind. Even if that were so, how important is it? The market for IT equipment responds to fashion rather than to its users' expressed needs; often this year's models are just different from, not better than, last year's. Again, with rare exceptions, no commercial or industrial user has ever succeeded in exhausting the capacity of the equipment currently available. The frenzied drive towards higher performance is fuelled by competition between suppliers, not by the frustrations of users. Experienced users have, indeed, been heard to plead for a pause to consolidate, for a rest from needless innovation. Moreover, it is the use, not the manufacture, of IT products that is important.

The sixth argument rests on a hidden premise, namely that because IT is now an essential component of the more lethal weapon systems it is necessary to be independent of all foreign sources of supply. It is less often expressed aloud because to do so may appear to identify potential enemies – among allies. That argument, however, is based not on economics but on national security, which is the subject of Chapter 7. Technological advance does indeed occur most rapidly under the spur of war, and in times of peace the needs attributed to national defence serve as a surrogate war. Moreover, the aims of the military coincide with those of the IT suppliers, for they also wish to maintain their competitive advantage in a market obsessed with technical performance. Research and development in IT is dominated by governmental spending on defence, and on the closely related needs of space flight. It is occasionally argued in support of this massive government expenditure that the resulting innovations 'spin-off' into the rest of industry. Even if that were true, it would still be an odd sort of way of using public money to promote economic health. A more direct approach would be cheaper and more controllable, although, without the political impetus given by defence, the funds would not be so readily forthcoming for research into IT.

We may doubt the doctrine of spin-off for at least two reasons. The first is historical. Britain was a successful electronic innovator in a war which she won, and has since spent heavily on defence. Japan has done neither, but one of the more striking economic consequences of IT has been the rise of Japan to become a leader in IT and other electronic products – not for nothing are these called the Sunrise industries. In part, that has been due to direct, deliberate and substantial governmental support for civil IT development. Again, large sums can be spent only by large organizations, but these rarely succeed in creative innovation; what they are best at is carrying forward the development of established ideas into effective, reliable and profitable products. Genuine novelty tends to emerge from smaller, less-disciplined groups, whose jaunty volatility can deny them the support of grave government departments and of larger users cast in the same too-cautious mould.

Getting and spending

Services based on IT are expected to expand as a part of a long-term trend away from heavy manufacturing in the industrialized West. What were the staple industries of the nineteenth century – steel, ship building and textiles – have declined as Western economies move into a 'post-industrial' phase[7]. That development has obvious implications for labour and for raw materials. It bears also on the demands for energy and transport, for heavy industry was a large consumer of these, but IT is not. Economic growth has become a fetish but economic policy lags on demand, and has its own inertia. The Western nations could find themselves over-provided with a still-expanding infrastructure of transport and energy supply that would have been needed to continue a super-seded pattern of economic growth. Worries about human safety and environmental pollution by coal-burning and nuclear power stations have given rise to a minor growth industry of their own in the form of endless public enquiries and the organization of protests. IT's displacement of the big consumers could curtail the need to expand the supply of energy, and provide a breathing space in which to map out a more acceptable path of development. Note 'could' not 'will': IT only enables, it never compels.

IT can be expected to reduce the demands for energy and for transport in other ways. Energy can be saved by advanced forms of automatic control, programmed to economize its use. More effective programs for the management of warehousing and distribution could reduce the needless transport of goods by a better anticipation of demand. Improved traffic control should reduce the waste of time and energy when moving goods and people, and there is scope for substituting telecommunications for commuting.

The application of IT affects the supply as well as the demand for resources. We have all read scare stories about the imminent exhaustion of coal, oil, metal ores or whatever, which are occasionally followed by reports of a major new discovery. Two facts are clear. First, our known resources are no more than those we happen to have found, which obviously depends on where we have looked, how hard, and with what equipment. So far we have merely scratched the surface of our planet; no one knows what exists down to, say, a depth of 5 km on land, and we are even more ignorant about what lies beneath the much larger area covered by the oceans. Second, what counts as a reserve depends on the price we are prepared to pay for it, and should current reserves really become worked out we can turn to those we call uneconomic – that is, more expensive, but not impossible to exploit.

The use of IT has improved both the location and the recovery of natural resources. The surveys used to locate new sources of oil and natural gas are based on analyses of seismic wave reflections from rocks lying deep underground, or beneath the sea floor. The pattern of reflections is exceedingly complex and few geologists are capable of interpreting it, but computer programs are now available to convert the confusing mass of observational data into clear maps of underground features. When such programs become part of the standard methods of analysis it is easy to forget that they promulgate only one theory of interpretation, if admittedly the best among current alternatives. There is a danger in this, and in every other analysis made by computers, that the assumptions behind the theory become fossilized and forgotten once they have been encapsulated in a successful program. The offshore rigs of the North Sea that exploit these discoveries rely heavily on IT for monitoring and managing their operations: dozens of data channels link them to the mainland.

We have noted already IT's role in controlling the launch of artificial satellites, and when these are equipped with optical and radio instruments they enable us to survey vast tracts of the earth's surface in a very short time. Satellites for survey work fly in orbits quite different from those used for telecommunications. To remain in fixed positions relative to the ground, telecommunication satellites have to be placed in a unique 'geostationary' orbit 36,000 km above the equator. Survey satellites fly in polar orbits, but their height is not critical, typically it is around 1000 km; as the earth revolves beneath the satellite it can scan the entire surface of the globe in about 250 orbits – about 400 hours.

The data collected is transmitted to a network of ground stations and processed by computers in order to present it in the form of coloured maps. These have been used by agricultural economists to map and monitor crops, and by geologists to narrow their fields of search by indicating areas that appear to be rich in oil or minerals. Pictures of cloud systems viewed from meteorological satellites are an everyday feature of televised weather forecasts. Accurate forecasts enable airlines and shipping companies to plan routes to save fuel and avoid storms, and they are invaluable to those who operate oil rigs in stormy waters.

Relevance and education

The rapid changes taking place in industry and commerce, in part as a result of applying IT, have raised questions about education. In Britain, schools and universities are frequently criticized for failing to produce men and women with the right qualifications. A commonplace excuse for poor economic performance is to say that our children's education is too 'academic', by being biassed too much towards the arts and literacy: and that it must be made more 'relevant' by biassing it instead towards numeracy and technology. British schools have, therefore, been equipped with small computers in the hope of correcting this defect. Children are now being taught to program badly by teachers who never learned to program well.

The next phase of attack is to complain that the school's equipment and its syllabus are each out of date. In part, such complaints arise from those who aspire to supply the deficiencies they claim to perceive. In part, they arise from the belief that, like Alice, IT finds itself in a Looking Glass Land where it is necessary to run to stay in the same place: a land in which innovation is endemic, and where last year's model is not merely superseded but is dangerously and misleadingly obsolete. Certainly, fierce competition between suppliers has enforced a frenetic pace of change, but most of it is cosmetic: the basic principles of IT do not change, and it is these that must be taught. It is easy enough to learn how to use the latest 'facilities', and it will, in any case, be necessary to do so at intervals throughout one's working life. On the job retraining will be a major and enduring feature, especially in the service industries, and is an activity in which IT will itself play a principal part.

Indeed, the only claim that technicalities can make to be a suitable subject for 'education', as opposed to 'training' in specific skills, is that studying them as examples to bring out their theoretical principles can be an adequate intellectual exercise, and one that can lay enduring foundations for the future. Training in practical skills is not to be despised, but they are essentially ephemeral. As Robert Hutchins remarked: 'The most practical education is the most theoretical'[35]. Practice passes, but theory remains. A firm grounding in theoretical principles will also provide a solid base on which individuals can rest their own critical evaluations of strident claims that the latest advance in IT is the long-awaited panacea for our economic ills.

Postscript

An uncritical use of IT adds to the risks of self-deception by tempting us to play the numbers game where it does nothing to advance our understanding. In particular, we believe ourselves to understand money costs, and we have been strongly conditioned to reduce them. We may even introduce them into situations where they are quite inappropriate by constructing artificial 'social costs' – for instance, the imagined costs of keeping motorists waiting in traffic jams. That is a harmless enough fancy until we direct our plans and policies towards social cost minimization; maximum social benefit is not the invariable result. Most accountants are tempted by a demon which drives them to cut costs at all costs; but a lean organization can also be a mean one, which fails in its primary purpose (and the only justification for its existence) which is to serve customers; it is then a rather small consolation that it fails to do so very cheaply.

Maximizing the measurable can also yield IT systems that are themselves highly 'efficient', but which overstress their users by treating them as mere system components with unvaried, untiring, instant responses. When computer terminal operators complain of eyestrain or backache they may well be using these specific and concrete symptoms to express less tangible discontents associated with 'computing stress'. That new industrial disease can be caused by monotony, by lack of control over the pace and organization of the work, and by a general feeling that operators are regarded as mere extensions of the machine, rather than being valued as complete human beings.

The broad effects of IT on economic activity have been seen by some of the more technically minded as ushering in 'the information society', in which information has become the principal object of economic activity. Two points may be made. First, we shall still need to be fed, clothed, washed and housed, so some basic agriculture and industry will remain. Second, information will not be itself the main commodity; rather IT will become an integral part of all products and services as these become ever more 'sophisticated'. It has also become a commonplace to speak of The Second Industrial Revolution, and those who do so urge us to avoid the social horrors they associate with the first one. The effects it had on working men and women were produced by concentrating production in urban factories, and by pacing them with untiring machinery driven first by water power and then by steam. The changes implied by the shift to service industries based on IT could be seen as a counter-revolution, for they offer the possibility of working at home, or in small dispersed units, and working at a pace determined by the operative rather than by the remorseless pulse of some central machinery.

Those of a romantic disposition, who yearn to return to the simple pleasures of a rusticity they never knew – without, of course, its dirt, disease or discomforts – welcome the opportunity that IT offers for cottage-industry decentralization. However, the very fact that IT enables us to connect, coordinate and manage a complex collection of dispersed activities means that it may come to be used somewhat less benevolently to concentrate and centralize economic and political power while appearing to disperse them: divide and rule is a familiar policy. Centralization is a matter of information flow, not of geography. What will happen depends on factors other than IT itself. It cannot be repeated too often or too emphatically that technology only enables, it does not compel (although in truth it also tempts). It by no means follows that, because some new thing can now be done, we ought to do it, much less that we must do it or perish. IT, like other technologies, provides the means, it cannot help us to choose the ends we ought to seek. Technological and economic factors commonly, and properly, have to give way before political considerations – as European agricultural surpluses show all too clearly. There can, however, be little doubt that IT is separating economic from political power by moving the locus of economic strength away from the smaller nation states towards the larger international corporations.

The principal economic problems we face are growth, inflation and unemployment. As we have seen, IT has contributions to make to economic growth by automation, and by its introduction of new products and services. Whether growth is a laudable social objective is another matter. The causes of inflation remain obscure, and IT cannot help us to do what we do not know how to do; although increasing automation is reducing the relative costs of some goods and services, including those of IT products themselves. The effects of IT on employment are taken up in the next chapter.

5

Productivity, IT and employment

More words have been written about the effects of computers on employment than on almost any other topic related to IT. The subject is one that attracts statistics as management and labour each strive to heap up evidence to overwhelm the other; but other people's statistics breed suspicion not trust. This chapter will not bury the subject under a mountain of obsolescent and disputable figures; it will attempt instead to present the principal factors involved.

No manager sets out with the prime aim of creating unemployment. The main reason for using IT is to reduce the unit cost of manufacturing some product or providing some service. When it is a matter of slimming a public bureaucracy, almost everyone speaks out fearlessly in favour of drastic economies. In other fields, senior managers find it prudent to present their cost-cutting proposals as ways of increasing productivity. That beguiling word makes it seems reactionary or irrational to oppose so eminently desirable an objective. Who can argue in favour of lower productivity?

Productivity is no more than a ratio of some input to some output, and measures the consumption of any resource used to create a product or a service. We can speak of the productivity of a raw material, or of a piece of machinery, but most often the word is used without a qualifying adjective and then refers to the use of labour. Thus, we measure the productivity of miners in tonnes per man-shift, or of typists in key-depressions per hour. Of course, productivity figures do not tell the whole story for nothing is said about the quality of the coal or the accuracy of the typing – let alone their usefulness. There is an unstated, but not always justified, assumption that quality has not been impaired by the acceleration of production. Experience has shown that most sustained increases in the productivity of labour have resulted from advances in technology. They have rarely demanded more physical effort and they have usually reduced the degree of skill involved, often to a trivial level. Typically, they have required investment in new equipment capable of being operated by fewer people to produce a larger output – the economist's classic substitution of capital for labour. For these reasons, productivity has increased most in prosperous industries with expanding markets.

The use of IT to increase productivity is not inherently adverse, for it can also improve the working conditions of those who do remain in employment. In manufacturing industry, from process control to assembly line, computers can be programmed to respond rapidly, consistently and calmly to changing circumstances and needs. They can optimize the adjustment of a tool or a process continuously, and by detecting the precursors of potentially dangerous situations they can initiate remedial action to protect the operators from injury, the plant from damage and the environment from pollution. Men and women can be relieved of hot, dirty, dangerous and tedious tasks. The investment in IT required to equip a large power station with automatic controls is tiny compared with its total cost, and would be much more than recovered were it to prevent just one unscheduled shut-down during the entire working life of the station.

In offices, the application of IT can relieve clerks of the tedious, subhuman, routine grind of keeping records and accounts, and it can free secretaries from the dreary chores of repeatedly retyping standard documents or oft-amended drafts. It can, also, relieve some of them of their jobs. The uncomfortable fact remains that, in industry and commerce IT's economic gains can be won only by replanning and reorganizing the methods of working, and entail redeploying and retraining at least some of the workforce, and may well enforce redundancy on others.

Productivity and employment

It is an obvious arithmetical fact, but one often glossed over, that increases in labour productivity imply a decrease in employment, unless output can be increased in at least the same proportion. There is no point in increasing output unless sales can be increased to absorb it. Productivity schemes are, of course, intended to reduce unit production costs and thus lower the selling price in order to tap new or larger markets, but that happy outcome is not always achievable. Success by one company is then achieved by undercutting its competitors and 'transferring' unemployment to them. Again, the headquarters of a business, or the offices of a government department rarely need to produce more memoranda or correspondence, but they will nevertheless install word-processors to cut office overheads by reducing the number of typists employed.

To take a third example, the numbers of journalists and compositors needed to produce a newspaper bears no simple relation to the size of its circulation. Their output is a single copy of the text and its setting-up for the presses. The introduction of IT enables the editorial staff to set up the type directly by using computer keyboards and display screens, and that, with the automation of the presses, very substantially reduces the need for skilled printers. This example illustrates rather starkly that productivity is not always a useful concept, for when, as here, a stage in the production process is eliminated completely, the productivity of its erstwhile workers rises to infinity as their number falls to zero. Their employer and his customers benefit from such a change, but those who have been made redundant are likely to take a more parochial view.

Automation can cut unit costs in various ways: obviously by enabling fewer workers to produce the same output, but also by producing a larger output with the same staff, or with a smaller investment in plant and machinery, or with less or cheaper raw materials. It can cut costs by reducing the number of defective units produced and rejected, and that has been its major contribution to the dramatic fall in the price of IT's own silicon chips, Alternatively, labour costs may be cut by reducing the levels of

skill and experience required, and that has enabled the manufacture of silicon chips to be transferred to low-wage economies
in Asia. Large increases in productivity have, indeed, been a
feature of the high-technology industries; in recent years their
output has increased but employment in them has fallen by an
almost equal proportion.

IT has not, of course, been the only or even the principal cause
of higher productivity. In British agriculture, for instance, more
food is being produced by a very much smaller workforce as a
result of simple mechanization replacing horses by horsepower:
better seeds, improved fertilizers and more effective pest control
have also played their parts, and it is only now that IT is being
applied to farm management and to make its machines 'smarter'.
Past advances in technology affected only manual workers, but
the impact of IT is more evenly spread. The lowest levels of office
work are little more than rigid routines which it was simple to
program and transfer to computer systems. Now that the easier
cuts have been made, attention is turning to the managerial
superstructure. One survey showed that, compared with their
American counterparts, British companies employ almost twice
as many managers per 'productive' employee [59]. Reorganization
and managerial redundancy are in early prospect.

Because the impact of IT is near-universal it is not possible to
make a useful global assessment of its consequences for employment. Any such attempt would be a simplistic guess, for the
effects of IT differ between different jobs, skills and experience,
and vary also with age, sex, education and social class. The
apostles of IT protest that its critics overlook the new jobs which it
generates, and argue that these offer the only secure hope of
replacing those lost in more traditional occupations. They add,
for good measure, that only IT can sharpen the competitive edge
of a nation's industry and prevent it from declining in world
markets. There is, however, little hard evidence that IT has in fact
created more jobs than it has eliminated. Nor is it likely that those
who are made redundant will have the appropriate education,
experience or aptitudes, or be in the right locations to take up a
new career in IT. The principal increase in employment in recent

times has been in part-time work for women in the service industries.

Automation and alienation

The social changes that accompanied the move from agriculture are recorded in numerous histories of the Industrial Revolution: they were, in part caused by the move of families from the countryside to urban slums. Industrialization imposed a division of labour in which the skilled work of an individual craftsman was broken down into a sequence of elementary operations, each of which could be performed by a semi-skilled machine operator. It was noted in 1848 that: 'Owing to the extensive use of machines and to the division of labour, the work of the proletarians has lost all individual character and consequently all charm for the workmen'[42].

'Charm' was putting it rather strongly, for the cold, wet, impoverished drudgery of a nineteenth-century farm labourer was no rural idyll; very few workmen – and even fewer working women – had much opportunity to experience the satisfaction that a craftsman derives from work well done. Intellectuals have always tended to take a romantic view of the dignity of manual labour. None the less, too single-minded a pursuit of efficiency by the automation of production can induce a sense of detachment or of feelings of alienation from the work, so that a job becomes no more than a man's or woman's current way of earning money.

Alienation is no longer confined to those on the factory floor, for many office workers have seen their work deskilled and paced, their responsibilities diminished and their status downgraded when an IT system was introduced. Insensitive system design can leave employees feeling that they are regarded as machine components, rather than that the system is there to help them as they perform significant tasks to which they bring their own unique contribution. Once it could be taken for granted that the senior staff of a company identified themselves with its aims and objectives; many today are very much less committed.

Western societies judge themselves and their citizens by economic criteria; someone's job determines their 'position' in society as well as their standard of living. Were alienation to become the norm, it could generate a sense of purposelessness, an attitude of irresponsibility, and eventually social unrest. Yet, there is nothing inherent in IT that forces us to develop systems which disregard the non-economic needs of men and women at work. In 1961, Pope John XXIII said: 'Every man has, of his very nature, a need to express himself in his work and thereby perfect his own being'. (No doubt the masculine was intended to embrace the feminine.) This is a matter that has also attracted the attention of psychologists, who have formulated the concept of 'job satisfaction'. They have discovered, to no one's surprise, that ideally work should interest, stimulate and challenge; that the worker should set the pace and see a meaningful end-product, should obtain fellowship and win respect for his or her achievement.

Some commentators react against the alienating consequences of automation by advocating a return to a simpler, rural, lifestyle. 'Green' parties and 'Ecology' movements have sprung up, but as yet they represent an untypical – and mainly middle class – minority of the population. It is entirely unrealistic to suppose that developed urban societies will make so drastic a reversal, or abandon innovation. What might be pleasant enough for an austere minority (in summer) would be impracticable for the mass, nor is there much evidence that the hedonistic majority would welcome it.

If we cannot eliminate alienation, we must seek to ameliorate it. One way to do so is to ensure that those who will be affected by a proposed new system participate in setting the specifications for its design, and in planning and overseeing its installation and operation. Their participation must be genuine, must be no token involvement. Nor should it be that kind of *post facto* consultation which simply seeks approval for what has already been decided upstairs, and set thereafter in concrete; that transparent manoeuvre has been tried and found wanting, indeed it makes matters worse. There must be real possibilities for adjustment and alteration without loss of face on either side. Training is necessary so that staff at all levels can understand the opportunities and the constraints faced by the designers; and the designers must participate in the training in order to understand at first hand the hopes and fears of those their system will affect.

No one should expect consultation to be quick, easy or enjoyable: on the contrary, it will involve endlessly boring and frustrating meetings. It will also cost more and take longer than dictation from on high: but it is becoming ever more necessary if damaging disharmony is to be avoided, and it is no more than our fellow men and women have the right to expect.

Job mobility and training

In the early part of this century, on taking up his father's trade the son of a craftsman could expect to use the tools and apply the techniques his father had used throughout his working life. Even in the factories, where workers did not own the tools they used, production methods had remained much as they had been for a generation or more. Today, tools and techniques become obsolete more than once during a working lifetime, and the pace of change continues to accelerate. In the words of Margaret Mead: 'No one will live all his life in the world in which he was born, and no one will die in the world in which he worked'[43]. The recurring demand for new skills means that we will all need periodic retraining. Our working lives may become a series of sandwich courses, with slices of education and training alternating with work and leisure, rather than being concentrated in a thick slab at the beginning. How thin the slices, and how many, will depend on the nature of our work, for some skills will decay into obsolescence much sooner than others.

Routine clerical work or production-line operations demand little skill, and seem likely to demand even less in the future, so that a change in these jobs may require no more than a cursory introduction plus a few hours of hands-on experience provided by the employer. In more skilled occupations, and in those deliberately planned with job satisfaction in mind, the slices will be thicker and less frequent. By using IT, the techniques pioneered in Britain by the Open University will allow workers to retrain at home. Courses may be organized by the worker's trade union, and perhaps paid for jointly by the union, the relevant employers and the individual. Men and women made redundant after more than a nominal period of service commonly receive financial compensation for their prospective loss of earnings. To encourage them to prepare for new work, it has been proposed that this compensation should take the form of a non-cashable grant which can be used only to pay for retraining.

Entry to the professions is regulated by institutions which award qualifying certificates after tests which assess the adequacy of a candidate's knowledge and experience. Up to now, such qualifications have been awarded for life and removed only for flagrant incompetence or gross misconduct. However, the pace of advance means that professional knowledge also becomes obsolescent within a decade, and the institutions will soon be forced to consider whether their members should be allowed to retain their qualifications unless they can demonstrate familiarity with the current state of their art. Such a change of approach would require the professional bodies to conduct refresher courses, or to accredit those run by others, and could be very salutory. As now, each member would no doubt be expected to pay for his or her own retraining. Keeping up-to-date is at present left to an individual's sense of responsibility, it is a matter of professional ethics not to claim more knowledge than you possess. Compulsory refreshment would reinforce the uncertain promptings of conscience, especially if continued qualification were to be made a legal requirement for holding a practising certificate in all professions, as it is in medicine.

Expertise and the professional

Galloping obsolescence is an occupational disease for IT professionals. And, it faces them as well as the members of more traditional professions with the challenge of expert systems, and of more modest attempts to encapsulate professional skills in program packages. These packages offer instant expertise. There are, for instance those which subject data to complex statistical procedures. They can be used to extract the significant variables from the mass, to investigate correlations, to project trends and so on. There is little reason to doubt that such packages apply their procedures correctly, but do they remove the need to engage a professional statistician?

Every computer program, long or short, packaged or tailormade, has its limitations; thus, it may assume that its input data will always be within specified limits, or that their values will range according to one of the more symmetrical distributions. Even where the data are those the programmer expected, the circumstances may not be well suited to that particular method of analysis. Known limitations of these kinds will be clearly declared in the operating instructions of any good package, but users read these only as a last resort, or they read them when they first acquire the package and promptly forget them.

Professional advice has its greatest value when things are going wrong, and no competitively priced package can hope to cater for all eventualities, even if its programmer were prescient enough to anticipate them. It is one thing to reach a certain result, quite another to assess its relevance, reliability and significance – to know what it really means. The naive use of advanced analyses by would-be instant statisticians causes little harm: the consequences of misapplying other forms of canned expertise could be more troublesome. Packages are invaluable for relieving an expert of the routine chores of analysis, or even those of design, but they must always be used with conscious care; they are sharp tools and can injure the unwary.

The value of an expert system derives from its success in extracting and encapsulating the data, methods and experience of specialists. It may be referred to as a knowledge-based system, but that title assumes a restricted definition of knowledge. Indeed, one of the problems faced by the designers of these systems is the collection and formal organization of human experts' understanding of their subject. Much of that lies below the threshold of conscious thought, particularly where value-judgments have to be made. IT systems can easily manage databanks of historical facts, but none is likely to write a good history – and neither are most men and women. Trained in the same methods and exposed to the same data, the better experts develop deeper insights into complex situations by subliminal processes which neither they nor anyone else understands well enough to program. Rules can be formulated and applied in straightforward 'normal' cases, but even the most pedestrian of professionals needs little help with them. Expert systems are tools for experts to use. They do not seem to me at all likely to cause unemployment among professional men and women, and their principal value may well lie in raising the average level of competence within a profession by supporting its weaker or less experienced members with a 'second opinion' available cheaply and inconspicuously from the best. Used in that way, they could also play an important part in training.

One of the more highly publicised applications of expert systems has been to medicine and psychiatry (Fig. 2). Very promising results have been achieved in the diagnosis of particular groups of diseases. Here the limitations of programming can be converted into positive virtues, for the formal, logical, plodding and exhaustive approach that these impose ensures that possibilities are not leapt over by human intuition, or missed through inattention, fatigue or lapses of memory. Indeed, the very act of converting expert knowledge into programmable form helps to reveal gaps, unsupported assumptions and inconsistencies, and thus stimulates research. That consequence was foreseen by Ada Augusta, Countess of Lovelace, in 1842[1], when she wrote about Babbage's Analytical Engine that, in order to make them more 'easily and rapidly amenable to the mechanical combinations of

Fig. 2. 'I need two of them in case I'm asked for a second opinion.' (*Courtesy of Sam Smith.*)

the engine . . . .[,] the relations and the nature of many subjects
. . . are necessarily thrown into new lights and more profoundly
investigated.'

The general use of expert systems could stratify a profession by
widening the gap between its more and its less active members.
Should that happen it will pose problems for the professional
bodies, for example, by exposing and increasing the tension
between their roles as protectors of their members' interests and
as guarantors of professional standards. They may be forced to
devise procedures for periodically assessing the continuing competence of individual members. It is never easy to strike a just
balance between rights and duties, and many professionals
will prefer to turn away from this thorny human problem and
immerse themselves in the fascinating technicalities of their
art.

The simple concept of productivity as an output/input ratio
does not fit most professional work. Certainly, by using the
programs and techniques of computer-aided design an engineer
can create a draft design for a bridge, or a silicon chip, in a much
shorter time. However, that facility is less likely to be used to cut
the labour costs of design than to generate and compare a much
wider range of alternative designs than would otherwise be feasible. IT's challenges to professionals are those of keeping abreast
of innovation, and of distinguishing between genuine advances
and mere fashion. IT will favour the more energetic and enterprising, although the governing bodies of the professions will
doubtless continue to urge that computer-based systems offer
expertise rather than experience, knowledge rather than wisdom
and, now and then, they will be right.

IT and the unions

The institutions to which professional men and women belong
regulate entry and set standards of behaviour. They have not
been much concerned with salaries or working conditions, or
negotiated with employers on behalf of their members. In part
this has been because the paradigm has been private practice in
which a professional advisor works directly to and for a client.

Today, most professionals are employees of large organizations, including governments, which with the 'industrialization' of professional and managerial work by the use of IT has stimulated the growth of in-house 'staff associations' to perform the traditional trade union functions. One result has been a debate about the conflict between collective fighting for rights and rewards and the individual's duty to uphold professional codes of behaviour. Those codes forbid striking, going slow or working to rule and some other kinds of industrial action which trades unions have long used to persuade obdurate employers.

That debate is irresolvable for there is a fundamental difference between the aims of a trade union and of a professional institution. The union's principal purpose is to advocate and protect the rights of its members: the institution's function is to protect the public from incompetence and dishonesty. That conflict has reduced the effectiveness of staff associations, many of which have been rather tame pussy cats that mewed pathetically but never bit or scratched. As a result, and largely as a consequence of IT, much more abrasive 'white collar' unions have emerged at the subprofessional level, and are recruiting upwards into the professions.

The received opinion is that trade unions are grimly opposed to innovation of any kind, and to the introduction of IT in particular. The myth is nurtured by the use of such emotive phrases as 'the impact of IT', or 'the resistance of the unions'. It is wrong to see IT as a battleground for economic war between workers and management, but that simplistic view will continue to be promulgated for, to take a phrase from a *Times* editorial, 'to put it at its lowest, the media's constant need for controversy makes sure of that'[(65)]. Luddite is a good word to enliven a headline, but it is only to be expected that those with long service in an industry will be concerned about threats to their investment in skill and experience, and about the uncertainty introduced into the futures of themselves and their families. They fear that their work will become less interesting, that it will be paced more exactingly, that some of them will be transferred and others dismissed. Traditional factory machines were immediately understandable as mechanized versions of familiar tools in which muscle power was replaced by steam or electricity. In contrast, IT, with its unbelievbably small and bafflingly silent silicon chips, and their disconcerting usurpation of mental functions, is much less cosy and many doubt their own ability to cope with its complexities.

Although trade union attitudes may not have been universally hostile, they have often been pessimistic, and reactive rather than creative – perceiving the use of IT as posing problems rather than as opening up opportunities. Unions have seen their members as threatened by four Rs: redundancy, redeployment, retraining and reduced skills. They have tended to respond with short-term opportunism, seeking to protect jobs and to win a share of the predicted productivity gains in compensation for accepting the inconveniences of innovation. But, they have also recognized that in the longer term the imaginative use of IT may be unavoidable if their jobs are to be preserved and their employers survive when faced by aggressively innovative competition. For this reason, a few unions have reached a new kind of understanding with employers in which a single union represents all workers in a plant, and its members agree not to oppose innovation with industrial action but to refer disputes to binding arbitration. In return, the employers agree to accept the arbitrator's decisions, to give their workers equal status with their managers in such symbolic matters as canteens and car parks, and to involve them fully in consultation about methods and manning before a new technology is introduced.

More traditional, and more politically motivated, unionists castigate these understandings as supine 'no-strike' agreements, and oppose them bitterly as throwing away a cherished union right, and as clever moves by cunning employers to emasculate their workers and charm them into a bovine docility. All established unions fear the loss of hard-won negotiating rights, status, and members as the skills they represent fade into obsolescence. So there have been attempts to 'black', that is to block, the introduction of new technology. As one committed socialist put it more nakedly than is customary: 'The employing class cannot work it without us'[29]. In a less miltantly class-conscious way, those working with new systems may do so apathetically, treating them as management's baby and rejecting all responsibility for interruptions or breakdowns.

Long experience has taught the workers that those who pay the piper call the tune, for rarely has a board of directors sat down to consider what changes they could initiate to improve the pay and working conditions of their employees. Their usual motive is economic; but what is seen as productivity in the Board Room appears as redundancy to the shop floor. When skills are made obsolete they are hardly ever replaced by new ones of any consequence, which means that anyone can then be quickly and easily replaced by anyone else. Management is attracted by the opportunity to replace skilled craftsmen with cheaper semi-skilled workers who are less militant, more easily replaced in case of disputes, and whose numbers can be increased or decreased at will to respond to short-term variations in demand. That flexibility for the workers is a reduction in their security of employment, and a degradation to the status of fully interchangeable homods.

Senior managers see IT as a means of reducing manufacturing costs, and of strengthening their control over the production cycle. However, their prime motives are economic not political, but to the workers and their unions the economic arguments are advanced as a decoy to deflect their attention from more significant changes in the organization of work. For them, the results of tighter management control are a fast, unremitting pace of working and an oppressive supervision over the amount and quality of an individual's output. Trade unions face difficult problems in seeking to deal with IT. They are weakened by divisions between unskilled labourers and skilled craftsmen jealous of their once-privileged position: IT blurs that distinction by making traditional skills obsolete. Again, local union branches have been organized plant by plant, but the consequences of IT ramify much more widely – at least to the company level, and perhaps to affect an entire industry.

The media have made merry in the past with who-does-what disputes between unions – should an engineer be allowed to drill holes in wood, or a carpenter in metal? More recently, the media have themselves provided a vivid illustration of inter-union conflict when IT revolutionized the production of newspapers. As

the first mass-production industry, printing has developed particularly strong and exclusive unions. To move ahead in the face
of prolonged opposition *The Times* (London) shut down its old
presses in Fleet Street, transferred production to a new plant on a
new site in Wapping, and by-passed the print unions by discharging its printers and employing electricians to run its new
electronically controlled presses. The electricians' union was not
opposed to that change.

Fleet Street had for so long been associated with newspapers
that this was seen as an audacious move, but it was not unprece-
dented. Employers in other industries have sought to break out
of similar deadlocks by transferring their operations to a new
work-force in a new place – 'green labour on a green-field site' –
and not always one in the same country, when the employer was
a multinational corporation. Trade unions facing a multinational
company need themselves to be organized internationally, or to
be able to mount a concerted approach by different national
unions. So far, neither the unions nor their members have shown
much interest or inclination for involvement in what is happening overseas. Moreover, in some countries, trade unions are
organized by crafts, in others by industry. The problem is a
difficult one, and IT's support for international business operations makes it more so, but it must be solved.

The example of Wapping is a partial answer to those who have
worried that the organization of IT workers into unions will
unduly concentrate economic and political power in the hands of
a minority, and who have feared that unions will recruit and use
IT staff as storm troopers in other disputes as well as their own.
The countervailing arguments are first that increasingly reliable
automation means that strikes will have less immediate effect as
systems continue to run with no more than occasional attention
from senior staff, and can be maintained by outside contractors.
Second that long-term disputes, which could indeed be very
disruptive given the ramifications of IT, can be dealt with by
substituting alternative labour belonging to a less-militant union,
or to none. That possibility is likely to be most effective in times of
high unemployment.

Clearly, it is far better to head off open conflict by engaging those who will be affected by some proposed new application of IT in consultation. For this to be honest it must take place before management's plans have hardened to the point where a substantial change would be seen as a loss of face. Otherwise the employees and their unions will see it as a cynical exercise in 'protest absorption' or 'damage limitation' – and both have taken place. The aim must be to take the maximum possible account of the needs, wants and skills of those who will use, or be displaced by, the new system.

It is very much easier to enunciate the need for consultation than to carry it into effect. It is bound to add costs, introduce delays, and involve many hours of tedious discussion. Moreover, it is not feasible to hold a referendum on every point of decision, and the problems of representation therefore arise. The local trade union officers and officials are obvious candidates to represent the workers but their training and experience may not have conduced to creative thinking. They tend to react *ad hoc* to proposals by others, and feel on safer, more familiar, ground when they are criticizing what management has proposed. They are much more used to negotiating about pay, gradings, job protection, health and safety than about the revision of skills or the reorganization of production. For these reasons it is important to involve the rank and file members of unions as well as their officials and some form of election has to be devised. Members and officials will each need some preliminary training before effective consultation can begin, but this must be handled with great sensitivity to avoid any suggestion that it is a form of covert indoctrination, a propaganda exercise. Consultation presents the unions with a dilemma: take part and you have to share the blame when things go wrong; stand aside and you condemn yourself to impotence.

Work sharing

No law of nature, not even one of economics, requires a man or woman to work for 40 hours a week, 50 weeks a year for 45 years: each of those numbers is negotiable. Indeed, the working week has shrunk from 65 to less than 40 hours over the last century or so. Naive arithmetic suggests that unemployment could be eliminated by a further reduction in the working week; or by longer holidays; or by extended training, even amounting to sabbatical years; or by earlier retirement – in other words by sharing around the work to be done. A first step might be to eliminate overtime working.

Work sharing has little appeal for employers engaged in manufacturing. Their wish is to reduce costs and it can be most immediately satisfied by engaging fewer workers for longer hours, and by working shifts to earn the maximum return on their investment in capital equipment. Overtime working offers flexibility, plus the evident advantages of using operators who are already familiar with the machines, processes and procedures in use. The trade unions, also, have reservations about the loss of overtime earnings, which have become a valued and significant part of their members' wages. Again, work sharing on the scale needed to cure unemployment would require a national redeployment of labour, with troublesome consequences for schooling, housing and social life. Movements between employers would erode a union's hard-won negotiating position. Transfers across existing boundaries between skills would blur the edge of demarcation disputes, and reduce the membership of particular unions, or force mergers between them. Wage scales would need to be coordinated to a degree that would disturb cherished differentials and relativities, and central direction would be unwelcome.

Clearly, work sharing raises substantial social and political problems; none of them requires impossible changes, but none is likely to happen quickly. Certainly none will happen at all unless the government forces changes on employers and employees alike, and few politicians see any votes in that. There has, however, been a spontaneous increase in part-time employment, particularly for women in the service occupations. With the rise of services relative to manufacturing, that trend seems set to continue. Part-time working is most popular in Britain, where it accounts for more than a fifth of the work-force – about twice the proportion found in other industrialized countries. It is popular also with employers who find that the low pay, flexible hours and ease of hiring and firing accepted by part-time workers more than offset the disadvantages of absenteeism, higher training costs and reduced continuity of service. Part-time working is also well suited to work that can be performed at home by using IT. The trade unions have expressed concern that part-timers are being exploited, and are peculiarly vulnerable to employer pressures, because few of them are organized to oppose unreasonable demands. In part, this is because most part-time workers are women, and women have never been strongly attracted to trade union membership. Also part-time jobs are seen by many as a casual supplement to a family income, rather than as a serious 'career', which had enabled employers to offer inequitably low rates of pay. The unions' difficulties are made no easier by the circumstance that many have more than one part-time job, and frequently change their employers.

Postscript

It would be quite easy to plot a graph or draw up a table of statistics to show that unemployment has risen as we have increased our use of IT; but it would be fatuous to draw any conclusion other than that each has continued to grow during recent years. The labour force also has grown; and increasing numbers of women have entered paid employment other than domestic service, continuing a trend which began when they were recruited as cheap labour for the dark satanic mills of the industrial revolution.

The causes of unemployment are obscure, obdurate and manifold. In Britain, the failure to match increased productivity with increased sales has been endlessly debated, and the most commonly suggested causes are the loss of colonial markets, and the declining competitiveness of British goods as a result of a failure to maintain a rapid pace of innovation. Some commentators trace that failure to inadequate investment in research and development arising from the reluctance of British financial institutions to wait for long-term returns, and their preference for safer short-term gains from overseas. And, too large a proportion of innovative effort has been side-tracked by the insatiable demands of defence. The energetic application of IT may help by what it can do to improve product design, but there is no escape between the horns of the dilema that using IT, or any other new technology, reduces the demand for labour; and not using them reduces competitiveness and so reduces the demand for labour.

Faced with the pressing and unyielding problems of unemployment, governments sit tight and hope for growth. Today, as traditional industries continue to decline, economic growth is confined to new ones, many of which either derive directly from IT or rely on it to add smartness to their products. In these ways IT has contributed a little to the reduction of unemployment; and so far the losses of jobs directly and unambiguously attributable to IT are relatively small. Only IT offers much hope for increasing employment under a *laissez-faire* regime. The alternative, *dirigiste*, approach of government action can take various forms; two examples will suffice.

First, the government can redirect its spending on research and development away from defence projects towards non-military products – instead of hoping that these will spin-off as beneficent by-products. Second, there is no early limit to the amount of work that *could* usefully be undertaken were public benefit to be adopted as the goal. There is immense scope for improving roads, sewers, health and education services, and so on, and so on. For my part, I do not expect either course to be followed as a long-term policy by British governments. Each involves work that would span more than one electoral cycle. Each appeals to governments of the left, and appals those of the right, and bipartisan continuity has gone out of fashion.

But do we make too much fuss about IT? Is it really so powerful an agent of change? Or are the economic and social changes attributed to it no more than the current phase of the industrial revolution which began with a massive shift from agriculture into manufacturing? Many assert that IT has pitchforked us into a second industrial revolution in which the production of goods is giving way to the provision of services of all kinds (shops, transport, communciations, public administration, finance, education and health care). In Britain, these services employed about as many men and women as did manufacturing in 1962, 13 years later twice as many. So substantial a change in the pattern of employment must have significant social and economic overtones, for many of the opportunities being created are semi-skilled, part-time, jobs for women. These are poorly paid and insecure, but many of the women who fill them accept the disadvantages because in large measure they represent no more than a disposable supplement to a family's income, and not a life-time occupation.

Unemployment is an international problem. It is particularly acute for that two-thirds of the world's inhabitants who live in the Third World, where its consequences are exacerbated by a relentless natural increase in population. The acceptance of contraception might be more effective than any known economic nostrum, but it and other remedies suggested by the affluent West raise sensitive issues of national culture and tradition, of religion and of self-respect. IT's consequences for employment are confined to the more industrial economies, between which it has induced some gains and losses. In the developing nations, IT's principal effect is expected to be to raise the levels of industrial technique and production by crash programmes of automation, and of technical education and training by the use of packaged programs and databases.

It is easy to fall into the habit of thinking of unemployment as a statistic, the value of one variable in an economic model, and to forget that for the individual men and women affected its rate is always 100%. For them, apart from the obvious loss of income, there is a sense of living in limbo as they wait for work to give meaning and structure to their day. Western societies are besotted by economic criteria, and to be unemployed is to be cut off from making a socially valued contribution, to be laid aside as useless. This sense of rejection is especially acute among young men and women who never have had a job since leaving school; and trade unions do not adequately represent the never employed.

For optimists, these are the temporary problems of a transitional phase, as we move away from the baleful influence of the Protestant Work Ethic, and enter an age of leisure. The more idealistic of them hope that 'culture' and community service, rather than a heedless hedonism, will take over from paid employment as the foundation of a worthwhile life; but culture and service are values which receive little attention in contemporary education. Others, more pessimistic, foresee only the development of work substitutes (Fig. 3), administered as social tranquillizers to calm and divert an alienated and restive population. It would be tragic if, by using IT, governments were to revert to the policy of the Roman emperors, with social-security payments as the bread, and umpteen channels of satellite and cable television carrying endless replays of professional sporting events as the circuses.

These large matters go well beyond our subject, and I have broached them only because the way in which we decide to use IT may well influence the course and pace of events. It may be comforting to pretend that IT only enables, not compels, and that we can choose what to do. But, who exactly are the 'we' who will do the choosing? How, and in what forum, will the questions be put for collective decision? I suspect in none, for, in the Western world at any rate, the development and use of IT are almost

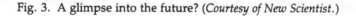

Fig. 3. A glimpse into the future? (*Courtesy of New Scientist.*)

certain to continue to go wherever the currents of commercial competition happen to carry them – and us.

Technologists are apt to protest that they are 'neutral artificers' who are not concerned with *what* should be done but only with *how* to do it more efficiently. So they may be if they choose to remain as mere mechanics, but those who aspire to professional status as they design IT systems must act at all times to ensure that they serve men and women, and not use them. They must use IT to increase the significance of work, and not to trivialize it; to introduce flexibility into working methods and timetables, and not rigidity; to develop human skills, and not to destroy or trivialize them; and to promote dispersal into small working groups, and not concentration.

It is my own belief that the most promising line of attack on the problem of unemployment is to be found in a combination of job creation and work sharing. IT has a part to play in job creation by improving the design of new products, and by contributing to the efficient control of complex public works launched – but not necessarily funded exclusively, by governments. Work-sharing on the necessary scale is also a matter for government action if the vested interests of employers and of those in employment are to be overcome. Sharing work is a way of increasing leisure and, to adopt a well-worn conceit, a man from Mars would be astounded to find the inhabitants of Earth opposing their release from laborious toil. But, a substantial increase in leisure without the funds to employ it in a satisfying way, or the education to make up for their lack, could just result in yet more time to kill: we will return to this point in the next chapter.

6

IT and the individual

Household chips

The high fixed costs of producing a new design of silicon chip and of programming a new application imply that one of the more profitable outlets for microcomputers is the domestic mass market. Few of us are aware that every day we use 30 or more small electric motors in our homes and our cars: in the same casual way we are coming to rely on an increasing number of small computers. These we throw away and replace as required for they have a single hard-wired program, and for that reason are often known as 'microprocessors' rather than as computers.

Household appliances such as cookers, washing machines, sewing and knitting machines are equipped with microprocessor control to sharpen their competitive edge. This does not make them 'intelligent', however hard advertisers may try to persuade us, but it does make them more effective and helpful – more competent, more smart. Household systems also are improved by microprocessor control. Central heating can be much more flexibly controlled than by a simple time-switch-cum-thermostat. With sensors in every room and remote control over individual radiators, independent heating cycles can be programmed for each part of a house to match its pattern of use, and to conserve energy overall. The room sensors can be more subtle than mere thermometers, measuring the balance between radiated and convected heat, and the movement and humidity of air. The control computer can be programmed to respond to combined evaluations of these readings in terms of human comfort and individual preference, and to take account of the special requirements of indoor plants, antique furniture, paintings and so on. Such a system is able to provide whatever refinement ingenuity may suggest or affluence afford.

Energy saving requires the heating system to respond to the rates of heating and cooling as well as to their absolute amounts, and to changes in weather and season so that, for instance, heat pumps and solar panels can be combined with an ordinary boiler to achieve an optimal result. Programmed control of the domestic hot water supply can match the input of energy to the predicted demand for baths, cooking and laundry in order to minimize the heat losses incurred by having too much hot water available too soon. However, the best performance can be achieved only by exercising much more forethought and planning than is usual in domestic life – more, perhaps, than many of us would find acceptable.

Microprocessors will be used increasingly to carry out simple safety checks. Leakage current meters reveal actual or incipient electrical faults, and the consumption of electricity could be monitored to ensure that lights and appliances are not unwittingly left on all night or during holidays. Sensors could detect escapes of gas from cookers, boilers or fires; water-flow meters could reveal burst pipes, leaking radiators or running taps. The domestic possessions of an affluent society offer tempting targets and need protection against theft. A variety of intruder alarms, from simple switches on doors and windows, or pressure pads in paths and corridors, to sonar, infrared and microwave beams guarding open spaces inside and around the house are easily monitored by a tireless and incorruptible chip. It could also control and time the recording of all calls to the telephone or at the front door. Individually programmed electrical bolts are more secure than mechanical locks, for the codes that open them can be easily and frequently changed by the householder. Cars and other movable valuables can be plugged-in to the house alarm system. The possibilities are endless; the problem is to decide what is worthwhile, what sales pressure may persuade us to acquire, or what insurers will require.

As well as these automatic-control functions, large numbers of personal computers are sold for straightforward calculation. They can keep the household income and expenditure accounts and perform financial calculations related to tax, insurance and investment. They can provide reminders about payments due, and monitor public utility and other regular bills by comparing them with corresponding periods in previous years to check for errors, or to highlight significant changes in consumption. They can operate a budgetary control system to ensure that future known commitments are met, and perform calculations for financing such major items of expenditure as exotic holidays, car replacement, or house purchase. Ordinary men and women who use these services soon become aware of the need for accurate, regular and complete inputs of data; for many of them that is an unfamiliar and uncongenial intrusion of rigour into the relaxing delights of domesticity. For most of us, also, our financial affairs are easily handled with a pencil on the back of a used envelope: it is self-control we need, not an unsleeping electronic accountant.

As well as acting as Treasurer of the Household, a personal computer can act as Domestic Secretary by maintaining records of correspondence, engagements and other commitments. Every member of the household could carry one of the quartz-watch-cum-diaries that are now available, and it would be plugged in to the domestic system overnight to exchange data, coordinate schedules and initiate reminders about the routine servicing of appliances and vehicles, licence renewals, subscriptions, appointments, anniversaries and so on. In this fashion our personal computers can serve us in ways that were previously available only to the very rich.

Communications

Even after allowing for differences in the methods used to sell them, it is not obvious why there should be so large a difference between the amounts that a typical family spends on motoring and on telecommunications. Few British households are equipped with more than a single telephone, and that is idle most of the day and almost all of the night. The communications element of IT is overdue for a major expansion into value-added information services.

Viewdata systems provide a telephone customer with a simple keyboard for interrogating central databases. So far, these have had only a limited success, and there are relatively few information sources; but there is no technical obstacle to providing worldwide access – although there is, of course, the question of cost, and there are political difficulties in some countries. By offering access to a wide range of information from alternative sources, and by allowing the enquirer to ask supplementary questions, viewdata could do much to counter the distortions inherent in editorial selection and reporter bias.

Viewdata shares with the teletext systems superposed on broadcast television the drawbacks of video-screen presentation. The amount of text and diagrams that can be displayed simultaneously is limited, the type-faces are barbarous, and the general effect is like reading a newspaper through binoculars – by candlelight. Again, in common with other personalized information services, viewdata presents only what we have asked to see; naturally, this is claimed as a virtue, but it does prevent us from acquiring, by the happy accidents of browsing, useful information that we did not know we wanted. However, as a new generation becomes accustomed to acquiring its information from an illuminated display rather than a printed page, as we accept the need to pay item-by-item for the information we use, and as the telephone companies move to providing it as a part of their standard package, so we will come to regard viewdata as a household necessity that we do not have to justify by using it for every minute of every day.

In most countries the postal and telephone systems are now separately managed, and the telephone companies are not allowed to use viewdata to provide an electronic mail service. The removal of that restriction cannot be long delayed, and will undoubtedly enlarge the average person's use of telecommunications. Their use of IT will also be enlarged by the marketing of automatic 'transponders' which *trans*mit or re*spond* to electric signals. With a transponder fitted to the domestic telephone we will be able to call our home number and then use the telephone dial or push-buttons to send a coded signal. The transponder will respond by repeating any messages received and recorded in our absence, and interrogate the domestic appliances and systems to check and report on their safety and operating status. It will reply in synthetic speech, and will be ready to accept coded commands to adjust the heating, start the cooking, and initiate a variety of remote control actions.

The household computers used to meter our consumptions of gas, water, electricity, telecommunication and information services will be connected to the same transponder, and will be used by the utilities to read their meters and present their bills, or automatically debit our bank accounts. Each would, of course, have access only to its own meter and be barred from any wider enquiry. All of this will take place by night to avoid clashing with our daytime use of the telephone, and the bell will be silenced to avoid rousing the household. By night also, the lines could be used to import and record items of news, instruction and entertainment which we have preselected, and can replay at will. The scope for the exploitation of IT in the home will be determined only by the length of our purse and our appetite for novelty.

Home education

As we have seen, education and training will cease to be a once-and-for-all initiation and will continue at intervals throughout our working lives and into our early retirement. Technical education will need to cut itself off from current practices and skills, and be founded on a more durable base of fundamental principles. Those who now cry for more 'relevance' in education are focussing short-sightedly on immediate gaps. There will always be specific narrow demands for retraining as practice changes, but there will also be a more important need for longer and broader periods of re-education to consolidate and extend our basic knowledge, and to prepare us for subsequent development. Methods are already available for remote learning, for instance those used successfully by the students of Britain's Open University. Sabbatical leave may cease to be an academic privilege and become the norm; if so, it would also help to fill some of the time left vacant by increases in productivity.

Computer systems are increasingly used to assist teaching and learning. Their video terminals can be adapted for use by disabled persons, and the blind will speak their questions and be answered by a synthetic voice – let us hope one that they can adjust to their taste. Programmed learning, or computer-aided instruction (CAI), takes pupils in planned stages through a mixture of instruction and tests, analyses their responses and presents again in an alternative form whatever has been missed or misunderstood. Pupils proceed at their own pace, and receive individual attention from an endlessly patient machine; moreover, the teaching methods and course material are prepared by the best available teachers. It is also possible for training purposes to construct a mock-up of the controls and instruments that will be used in some new plant or process, and to connect these to a computer which has been programmed to simulate its operation. This has proved to be invaluable for training pilots to fly a new aircraft, and it allows both normal and emergency situations to be presented very realistically so that pupils can learn to cope with them in stressful circumstances, but ones in which they can harm neither themselves nor the plant.

CAI emphasizes the acquisition of knowledge: it is the equivalent of studying an interactive textbook. The use of simulation plus evaluation has the more ambitious task of achieving understanding by computer-aided learning (CAL), for it encourages pupils to deepen and enlarge their knowledge by surrogate experimentation. Engineering students, for example, can investigate the behaviour and failures of alternative models of large systems or structures that would be much too expensive, too dangerous or too time consuming to construct for testing. This enables them to experience at first hand the exciting and exasperating challenges of creative original design, rather than being confined to critical analyses of textbook examples. Medical students can sharpen their diagnostic wits on simulated patients, and cover the widest possible range of diseases and a variety of misleading complications.

Computer-aided learning and instruction are each in a primitive stage of their development. Their disadvantages include the temptation to propagate a single point of view, for the high costs of producing a new course favour the widest possible use of the 'one best' program. Moreover, the use of a computer in a sensitive tutorial role is a seductive and insidious way of conditioning students to accept the mores of technological culture.

Whatever may be its merits for general education, computer-aided instruction and learning do enable us to study at home at times to suit ourselves. At first, it seemed likely that home education would be based on large central computers each serving many remote students sitting at viewdata terminals. However, the technology now allows us to store many hundreds of megabytes of data or programs on a single compact disc of the kind developed for sound recording. An alternative technique employs an optically recorded video disc to store still or moving pictures, sound, text and control programs. One example of such a disc holds 4000 still pictures, 160 film sequences with sound, and 100 kilobytes of data and control programs. It is used interactively to simulate the management of the nature reserve at Slapton Ley in Devon, and it can be regarded either as an instructive simulation, or as a testing intellectual game[48].

The initial, fixed, costs of producing such a disc are very high, but the marginal cost of pressing one extra copy is trivial. Given a mass market, plus the availability of cheap personal computers, compact discs offer a low-cost, convenient alternative, which frees the telephone line for other uses. Just one such disc can hold 100 million words – the text of almost a thousand books, and the techniques of information storage are nowhere near their limit. A few discs could hold a library large enough to frighten anyone; but they could also hold the librarian, in the form of programs to guide enquirers' searches for information, and help them to interpret and evaluate it to enhance their understanding.

Medicine

Successful medical treatment requires timely and accurate diagnosis, but in almost every country there are too few doctors. Poorer people also are reluctant to initiate a process over which they soon lose control, and which they fear may sweep them into lengthy and disruptive courses of treatment which will reduce their earnings. Trained paramedics can help by making preliminary examinations of a much larger number of patients, and filtering out those whose problems appear to be serious. They are making particularly valuable contributions to health care in the less developed countries, but considerable scope exists for their wider use in the Western world also.

There is no reason why personal computers should not eventually be equipped with expert medical programs for pre-medical screening. They are already being used in hospitals to conduct the usual initial interviews in order to ease the pressure on doctors' time. Those quizzes will be further helped when smart cards come into general use and carry our medical histories, plus vital data on blood groups, drug allergies and so on.

The range of non-invasive scanning techniques that have become popular rely heavily on IT to present their data pictorially in order to assist surgeons. IT also assists anaesthetists to monitor the vital functions of those who have the misfortune to find themselves on the operating table; and it helps nurses by watching over patients in intensive care, doing so unsleepingly, without distraction or fatigue.

Electronic devices are beginning to help those with mental or physical handicaps. Artificial limbs are more responsive when computer-controlled, and ingenious means have been devised to assist even quite severely handicapped persons to read, to operate keyboards or to play musical instruments. The scope for treating mental handicaps by audio-visual displays responding to the patient's alpha-rhythm and other forms of bio-feedback remains to be explored. In these, and in other ways too numerous to list, IT is contributing to medical treatment. We can welcome this demonstration that the social and personal implications of the new technology are not irredeemably bad, but we must not allow the practice of medicine to become industralized. Men and women cannot be reduced to standardized assemblies of interacting psycho-physiological systems. Patients already dislike the hospital environment, and would be even less happy in one dominated by an incomprehensible high technology. We need to be treated as the unique individuals we know ourselves to be, to feel valued for our own sakes, and when we are ill to be cosseted by the time-tested method of 'tender loving care'. Successful medical treatment needs more than artificial intelligence, it needs natural human understanding.

Leisure

A reduced working life, whether it results from increased productivity or economic decline, implies an increase in free time. Not all of it will be leisure, some is more accurately described as 'non-working time'. A shorter working week has often meant the same number of hours being spent at work, but more of them being paid at premium, overtime, rates; for a negotiated reduction in standard hours may be a cosmetic disguise for higher pay. A shorter working week also provides an opportunity to moonlight, to work at a second job, to increase one's cash income. Again, many of us, faced with ever-rising charges for personal and domestic services, have taken to decorating and repairing our own houses, growing our vegetables and performing other chores which we would once have paid others to perform for us. In each case, the earning or saving of money has been preferred to the enjoyment of leisure.

In practice, not everyone welcomes the prospect of increased leisure: for some, freed time is an imposed vacancy in which to be idle and bored. Unfortunately, this may most often be so for those likely to be displaced or downgraded by automation, or who never have been employed. They tend to be those who have been ill prepared by their education to occupy themselves, and who lack the money to pay for the increasingly sophisticated and expensive products of the 'leisure industry'. Alienation or rejection at work combined with boredom at home is a recipe for social unrest, especially among the energetic young who have little to lose. How ought they to fill the leisure which IT-induced productivity has thrust upon them? Should they seek to use their leisure to compensate for the opportunities denied them for self-expression through work? Ought we all to use our leisure to enlarge, and not to degrade our personalities?

'Ought' is a normative word which, with such phrases as 'the right use of leisure', has overtones of Victorian paternalism and 'do-goodery'. Those who write about other people's use of leisure always want to fill it with improving activities of the kind they themselves would enjoy – usually highish-brow culture. But, in what sense can it be said to be better to read a literary classic rather than to leaf through the comics? Why is it thought better to play chess in a club than darts in a pub? Is it really better to be active rather than passive – to play indifferent amateur football rather than watch the professionals on television? Those who argue that neither primary nor secondary education does anything like enough to prepare us to fill our leisure in 'worthwhile' ways commend all forms of further education for adults from evening classes in woodwork to extra-mural degrees in biophysics. Their critics comment sourly that there is little evidence to show that those who engage in intellectual or aesthetic activities are happier or more socially valuable than any others. More politically minded critics dismiss all such remedial proposals as élitist, and see them as condescending attempts to direct the free activity of adults as if they were children. Some, who enjoy conspiracy theories, even see these as crafty attempts to divert discontented workers from plotting social change.

Western societies no longer have accepted sets of values, and discussions about the use of increased leisure degenerate into debates between parties who share no common ground. That barren situation has been attributed to the decline of religious belief, to the aftermath of war, or to the rise of a greedy consumerism. The development of IT may itself have contributed in more recent years because its goals and its criteria have been overwhelmingly technical and economic. In hot pursuit of their employers' interests, IT system designers have emphasized quantitative data and results, and devalued qualitative facts and emotional needs by ignoring them. The great prestige of science (before the Bomb) led to the neglect of human virtues and values, for its boasted objectivity and universality derived from its exclusion of the subjective. Ironically, once expelled with a pitchfork, human nature has re-entered modern physics with a vengeance. Technology, however, tends to employ yesterday's science and when using it we need to take great care to ensure that we do not conceive too narrowly the consequences we plan for men, women and society – nor overlook others we did not intend. This is especially true for IT, whose applications pervade every aspect of our lives – domestic as well as social, political as well as economic.

Perhaps the only value-judgment likely to command wide acceptance is that individual men and women are important in their own right; few regimes or ideologies openly deny that view. We should, therefore, seek to help people to realize their own potential in their own ways, whether at work or at leisure, so that they do not decline into the sad syndromes of listlessness or alienation. Our education must provide the basic skills we need for that purpose; above all it should teach us how to learn, and how to exercise an independent critical judgment. That last we need to counter the high-powered presentation by the media of stereotypes of wealthy leisure-class behaviour as if these were models worthy of our emulation. We cannot all live like the feckless few in the commercials, and it is needlessly provocative to suggest to the underprivileged that they can.

IT and art

As leisure activities, the arts and crafts are esteemed for the skills they require, and recommended as therapy for the boredom and stresses of urban life. They may appear to have little to do with IT, although intrepid men and women have programmed computers to write 'music' and 'poetry', and also to paint and draw. Their programs have used the basic rules of the art to direct a computer's output, and have relied on random numbers to introduce unpredictable changes at branch points in the program in order to generate undetermined results. Those are then filtered to reject the ones that fail whatever criteria the programmer has adopted to distinguish art from doodling. There is the crux. It is all too easy to create uncontrolled and unexpected output; the problem is to identify that tiny fraction of it with any pretension to artistic merit. G. K. Chesterton once wrote: 'Art is the signature of man'[17], but men and women have never agreed how to separate art from rubbish.

Computer art is one thing, computer-aided art is another.

Computers can drive printers and plotters to produce coloured graphs, maps and diagrams; and can produce mosaics of coloured spots on a video screen. The position, colour and brightness of each spot (each picture element or 'pixel') is represented by numbers which the computer can process to change the picture. Ingenious programs make the image appear to rotate as if on a turntable, or wrap it around a complex shape, or shade it for oblique illumination, and so on. The walls of the computer departments in most universities are decorated with fading tracings produced by playful programmers or ingenious mathematicians. Even a small personal computer can be programmed to cause a television set to display on demand straight lines, polygons, conic section curves and so forth, and to do so in whatever relations and colours, and in this way to generate patterns and pictures at will.

Again, a microprocessor can be used to provide a simplified keyboard control for difficult musical instruments, and so to reduce the skill needed to play them. Used with an electronic sound synthesizer, such a computer enables an amateur to compose music and edit out mistakes of composition or execution. In such ways we can cater for those who, although they differ greatly in competence, are equal in their need for creative activity. IT acquires unambiguous social merit when it is used to enable the mentally or physically handicapped to enjoy the pleasures of an executant's performance in the musical or the graphic arts, and yet is able to do so without making it so simple that they provide no opportunities for skill and self-expression.

But we have a most unfortunate capacity for developing a splendid technology and then frittering it away on inanities – consider colour television. IT has not avoided that folly; it is being used to bring the video games and gambles of the amusement arcade into the home, with their undesirable assumptions about the acceptability of vicarious violence. These are, indeed, the principal, and in many cases the only, use made of the personal computers which have been sold in their hundreds of thousands to mop up the surplus capacity installed for the manufacture of silicon chips, rather than to enhance the quality of our lives. Simulators of the kind used to train airline pilots will almost certainly appear in the fairground and the amusement arcade. They will not be limited to visual displays, but will enable customers to experience all the thrills of piloting *Concorde*, controlling a bob sleigh, or riding a racing motorcycle without risk to life or limb. Experiments with rats have shown that it is possible to feed an electrical stimulus directly to the part of their brains which controls the sensations of pleasure. Offered the choice between a pedal to produce pleasure and one to release food, even hungry rats did not hesitate, they were hooked on pleasure. I find it hard to believe that an addiction of that power will not be exploited commercially for human use, unless we choose to legislate to ban it as a form of electronic drug.

Why travel?

The telecommunications functions of IT challenge our need to travel. Videotex systems can bring into our homes the electronic equivalents of mail-order catalogues of tens of thousands of items – all 'unrepeatable' offers and lotteries. Their advertisements, moreover, will be screened for as long as we are prepared to endure them rather than for the few seconds allotted to a television commercial. As well as goods, we will be offered financial and other services, holidays, sports and entertainment. Payment will be by direct-debit cards, with funds being instantly, silently and painlessly extracted from our bank accounts. For retail sales, hypermarkets will give way to 'telemarkets' delivering to their customers from automatic warehouses, or more probably parcelling goods for customers to pick up at collection points. Only in the realm of science fiction is it possible to dematerialize goods and transport them electronically, but it is feasible to send programs to control automatic tools. For example, spare parts for aircraft or automobiles need not be carried physically to remote places when it is quicker and cheaper to send the programs to control machine tools which can make them in small quantities on the spot and as required.

Shopping, however, has social as well as economic functions. It provides an opportunity for the members of a community to mix, for friends to meet informally, for exercise and for pleasant occupation. Many of us would miss these benign side-effects. No one would regret the passing of hypermarkets, for they rarely advance the art of architecture or enhance amenity, but if tele-shopping were to lead to the decline of more traditional shopping and the closure of small shops it would have most unwelcome consequences for the appearance and activity of town centres.

In the form of videotex services, IT could encourage the growth of common-interest groups – 'invisible clubs', for instance a group of chess players. These would be particularly valuable for the immobile elderly and the disabled. Costs apart, such groups could establish informal cross-linkages between individuals in different countries, and those could produce significant and beneficial changes.

The scope for working from home, using a terminal provided by the employer, has been much discussed. This 'telecommuting' would undoubtedly save a great deal of time, temper and energy which is now dissipated in travelling to and from work. In city centres, noise, pollution and congestion would all be reduced. The physically handicapped can be helped, and women can work from home when their children are young. Prisoners could use terminals to work from their cells, in preparation for their return to normal life. Many office jobs depend on the processing and exchange of information rather than on being physically present at some particular place of work. Working from home is also well suited to freelance programmers, writers, market researchers, financial analysts and other kinds of consultants.

However, the fact that we have been slow to exploit the decentralizing potential of traditional telephone and telex services does suggest that there are human and social reasons for herding together at work. Indeed, an American study revealed that many would not like to work from home[52]. It was, of course, the rule for craftsmen before the Industrial Revolution of the last century gathered workers into factories, but the habit of 'going to work' has become ingrained, and today's homes have not been designed to cope with full-time occupation by all members of the family. Only the larger houses and apartments have space which could be used for working without domestic interruption or distraction. As with shopping, many men and women enjoy interacting with others outside their family circle, at work and even on their crowded journeys. The loss of those opportunities for wider contacts would reinforce the trends that already exist towards the fragmentation of the community into separate individuals. Terminal isolation would be a most regrettable social change[25,54]. Professional men and women can most easily work from home, and many already do so, but even they can be cut off from the easy, unforced exchanges of ideas with their peers, the stimulating criticism of their colleagues, and the casual office gossip over the coffee cups which keeps us in touch with what is happening outside our own small patch.

IT offers facilities for 'teleconferencing' which enable meetings to be held without the need for the parties to travel in order to assemble at one place. Enthusiasts have suggested, rather wildly, that this heralds the demise of the business trip abroad, and will thus save much time and money. That naive view ignores the prestige attached to foreign travel, and the relief it affords from the daily grind. Moreover, for the more crucial meetings it is extremely doubtful whether the suspicious would willingly forgo the opportunity to look into their opponents' eyes; and those blessed with dominant personalities will never abandon the face-to-face encounters which serve them so well. At the junior level, ambitious men and women will continue to want to be seen and known at central headquarters where the power resides. On the whole, it seems likely that teleconferencing will be most used for sales presentations, and by the more retiring academics as a means of conducting leisurely running arguments without the embarrassments of physical confrontations.

In contrast, IT is converting the busy executive's journeys by car or plane into extensions of the office. Communication satellites and cellular radio provide continuous telephone and data links; lightweight computers and compact discs provide portable private files and the means to process them. Spoken inputs and outputs, electronic navigation, collision radars, and safety checking will guide the vehicle automatically to its destination, freeing the passengers, and to some extent the drivers, to advance their personal careers. The personal computer can receive and store messages, and could perhaps be programmed to generate appropriate return signals to simulate a considered response, while exhausted travellers continue to catnap or attend to the variety of distractions provided in their 'moving information and entertainment space' – for it will no longer be advertised as a mere vehicle.

Telemarkets and the loss of the custom of office workers could lead to the decline of city-centre shops. The emptying of office blocks would also have a drastic effect on urban life and on town planning, as well as slashing the profitability of city road and transport systems. We must not allow the logic and economics of IT to mutilate our towns; it is essential, as in all applications of technology, to examine the wider consequences and not just the benefits for its immediate users. Yet harm is not inevitable; megalopolis could be divided into self-contained, human-scale, units – although that is not at all likely to happen spontaneously if it is left to the uncoordinated ambitions of individual entrepreneurs.

Telecommuting could be used to bring valuable job opportunities into rural areas and to remote islands, and so to help to check the emigration of young people in search of work. This could be achieved without the loss of social contacts by setting up work centres in villages and small towns. Equipped with communications and terminals, small computers and compact discs, they would operate as agencies performing work for a number of different employers. The employees would gain the benefits of human interaction, and work within walking distance; the client employers would avoid the costs of city-centre accommodation, and the centre's work-force could be flexibly deployed between clients to cover seasonal and occasional peaks and troughs.

Postscript

Any attempt to describe the many ways in which IT is impinging on the lives of ordinary men and women is apt to degenerate into a long and boring list of the latest gadgets and gimmicks. There is the further risk of portraying a technologist's paradise, in which 'intelligent' robots do all the work while serene and graceful men and women occupy themselves with philosophy and the arts. We know it will not be like that: nor would most of us enjoy so sterile an existence. Undoubtedly our use of IT will be accompanied by human and social changes, but many of these would have occurred anyway. IT's action will be to press some changes forward more rapidly by providing cheap and powerful instruments and systems.

Given that IT is providing us with an effective agent of change, we must take great care to see that it does not – by our neglect – determine the end as well as supplying the means. At present, no one seems to be choosing what society wishes to achieve through the development and application of IT, or what priorities should apply. There is a great number of individual projects, but no overall plan. Perhaps we should welcome this as a safeguard against rapid and sweeping changes initiated by uncritical enthusiasm. Social planning is only intermittently in favour in Western democracies, and when it becomes so the newly elected government has stored up many projects with more clamant claims on its attention than the planning and use of IT. None of the principal political parties attaches much real importance to IT.

The absence of any coherent strategy for guiding the developing use of IT makes it all the more important to monitor and evaluate what is actually happening unplanned. Otherwise we could suddenly find that the tide has been advancing remorselessly and has eroded the foundations of our sandcastle while we were diverting ourselves by playing with our new electronic bucket and spade.

The most important topic discussed above is education, and we have considered only briefly how IT can improve the mechanics of learning at home. The vital question for education is not 'how?' but 'why?' Are we aiming at raising the standards of culture? Or only at economic advance? Are we educating to live, or only to earn a living? IT, as such, does not affect that large decision, but its insistent demand for continuing training to keep abreast of the opposition does direct our attention away from, say, literature and the arts. And as it supplants traditional methods of learning, so it rivets our attention ever more securely to the omnipresent video screen as the true source of all knowledge. In Britain, two families in three never buy a book; and, on average, British children watch television for more than three hours each day. This narrowing of the range and variety of materials available, as compared with libraries, places far too heavy a responsibility on those who choose and shape video material. Their product too often blurs the distinction between fact and fiction, between say a realistic war drama and a filmed report from an actual battlefield. Often, also, the news is distorted by the severe selection and compression needed to fit it into a 15 minute slot, and is trivialized by interlarding it with vapid magazine items presented as of equal importance.

A plea for 'culture' need not conflict with the pursuit of prosperity; it is after all what we seek to achieve by our economic struggles – apart from dry beds and full bellies. By enlarging our perspective, and developing our critical faculties, education offers our only long-term hope of protection against the abuse of power, by enabling us to see through the pretensions of advertising, propaganda or fanaticism, and it is the only secure way to preserve a free democratic society. Even so, it would be facile to imply that education is the sovereign cure for all our social ills.

The changes and the risks sketched above relate to the affluent industrial countries of the northern hemisphere, or the Western democracies. They do not yet impinge on the majority of the world's population, for whom subsistence is much more important than high technology. For them, as individual men, women or children, IT is wholly irrelevant. Certainly it could be used to pump up the standard of living by making good their lack of industrial skills and accelerating the pace of economic growth. But, at the same time, it would import the economic and technological criteria which dominate – and distort – the education and culture of more developed countries, and few would claim that these enhance the human condition. IT offers no panacea for social or economic ills, yet it is not inherently evil. The changes that will come about through its agency will depend on the motives, the foresight and the compassion of those who promote and apply it, and only the incurably sanguine could believe that nothing but good will follow the unplanned and uncontrolled injection of IT into the less-industrialized nations.

7

Safety and security

It is convenient to consider the ways in which IT may be used to threaten or to protect the safety and security of our lives and property under four heads: safety of life, invasion of privacy, crime and war. Malign intent is not the principal reason for concern in the Western democracies, but risks can arise when IT systems themselves are faulty. In the early days, failures were mainly caused by hardware breakdowns; today, silicon chips are highly reliable, and the emphasis has moved to data errors and software 'bugs'.

Input data may be incorrectly scanned by automatic readers, and human operators make mistakes when entering data through a keyboard; checks are therefore made to reveal the presence of errors. The simplest, but not the cheapest, check is for two independent operators to enter the data and then to compare their versions; if they agree then it is highly likely that no mistake was made. Otherwise, the entry is repeated until they do agree. Or, a batch of items of numerical data may be added together on a pocket calculator and the total entered as a 'sum check' to be compared with the result of the same addition by the computer once input is complete. It is not necessary for the total to have a meaning. Thus, the birth dates of a group of staff can be totalled for comparison; such a total is known as a 'hash total'. Some input errors are gross enough to be exposed by a 'credibility check'; for instance, no date requires a month of more than 31 days, and no employee can work for more than 168 hours in one week.

Data may be lost or corrupted in transmission over cable or radio links when electrical noise and interference are picked up, when disconnections or other faults occur, or when maintenance engineers are working on the equipment. Many techniques are available for preserving the 'integrity' of data communications; they range from methods of handling the electrical signals them- selves, to clever ways of encoding the data so that any errors introduced in transit can be detected, or even corrected automati- cally, provided that they do not occur too frequently or too close together. Again, the computer may be programmed to send periodic test messages to discover whether the channel is suf- fering noise or interference, and to suspend or duplicate trans- mission when acceptable limits are exceeded. All this checking for errors, this 'data vetting', absorbs computer time and costs money; but experience has shown it to be essential, and a nice balance has to be struck between the decreased risk of undetected errors and the increased cost of checking.

Data can also be lost or corrupted in the processes of storage and retrieval inside an IT system. Magnetic storage media can be affected adversely by dust, heat and humidity, and high-speed electronic stores can be upset by power failures and electrical disturbances, or even (but rarely) by cosmic rays. The remedies are two-fold. First, remove the cause by using air-conditioning to extract dust and to control temperature and humidity, and by fitting electrical filters and voltage regulating circuits to smooth the power supplies. Second, as for data transmission channels, to use error-detecting or error-correcting codes.

In Europe, the USA and Japan, electrical power is generated at many independent sites and distributed over national networks which offer alternative routes: even a major failure, such as the loss of a generating station or a power line, can rapidly be made good by redeployment. Most losses of power are the result of local breakdowns, lightning strokes or human errors, and rarely last for more than a few minutes. They can be bridged by using standby batteries to maintain an emergency supply to the more important units of an IT system. Breaks lasting for several hours, or even days, may occur as a result of unusually extensive failures of equipment, major fires or severe storm damage. They could also be caused by strike action during an industrial dispute. To cover these longer interruptions a local source of power, commonly a diesel- or petrol-driven generator, is used to charge the standby batteries.

Emergency power supplies add to costs; they must also be properly maintained and regularly exercised to ensure that they, and those who operate them, remain effective. Hence, they are installed only for computer and telecommunications equipment whose continuous operation is exceptionally important – for example, those concerned with national defence, or with safety of life. Different IT systems are affected differently by prolonged power failure; moreover, an emergency supply can last no longer than its fuel reserve allows; hence, when designing a new system the appropriate degree of protection should be evaluated realistically. At times of lengthy power failure, many users will compete raucously for fuel and for generators, and it will then be too late to obtain what should be provided from the outset.

Errors in programs, more commonly called 'software bugs', are of three principal kinds. First, logical errors, where the programmer has made a mistake in the analysis of a process. Second, syntactical errors, where an instruction is erroneously expressed in a way that breaks the rigid and formalistic rules which govern most programming languages. Most of these should be thrown out automatically for correction when the program is being compiled. The third type includes transcription errors caused by a mistake in copying, or in the input of the program.

A major program contains many thousands of instructions, some of which are conditional jumps that select the route through the program which matches whatever data and circumstances it happens to meet during execution. Commercial programs have a particularly high proportion of these jumps, and the total number of alternative routes that they provide is so very large that it is simply not feasible to examine and test every possible combination. Even after several months of trouble-free operation we cannot be sure that every nook and cranny in the program has been explored. It is not possible, therefore, to be absolutely certain that a program of realistic size is ever free from error. This doubt, moreover, applies not only to users' programs but also to the computer's operating system, which controls the execution of every other program processed by the system. Large programs seem to reach an equilibrium in which the acts of searching for and correcting errors introduce about as many new errors as they remove. Debugging is an art and a chore which absorbs a great deal of programmers' time and, because it depends on detective flair, individuals who are equally intelligent and equally well trained differ very considerably in their ability to debug.

A program may be reasonably free from errors but unsuitable because its system designer failed to meet its user's needs either by specifying inadequate or inappropriate procedures or by failing to foresee and provide for all possible combinations of circumstances. Again, the operators in a computer centre may mount the wrong program tapes or discs, or give incorrect commands from the control console, or make other mistakes through lack of skill, inadequate information, pressure of work, or sheer carelessness. Fortunately, most such errors produce obvious nonsense and the system 'crashes'; work is halted and the only penalties are costs and delays.

In these various ways, an IT system can give rise to errors or fail to match the expectations of its users. Most often these failures and inadequacies cause no serious or irreparable damage, or the damage is limited to a particular user who has to pick up the pieces. When, however, the consequences of failure are more serious, or more widespread, it becomes desirable to double-check the system design, and independent experts may be called in to conduct an 'integrity audit'. For example, we might reasonably expect such an audit to be a prerequisite for an IT system which is to control air traffic, or one intended to monitor and regulate the operation of a nuclear power plant.

Safety of life

The uses of IT in medicine have been mentioned above, and we noted its contributions to the improvement of scanners, to anaesthesia and to the nursing of patients under intensive care. Smart cards will add to our protection in cases of accident or sudden illness by carrying records of our medical history, our blood group and any drug allergies. IT is being used by the fire and ambulance services to enhance their communications, to record the locations of special hazards and to plan the deployment of their resources.

By reducing delays, ingenious systems of traffic control based on models of vehicular flow can improve the tempers of impatient drivers and thus lessen the risk of accidents. Drivers are also being alerted to known hazards by motorway signs illuminated automatically when fog or icy roads are detected. Near major international airports, air-traffic control would be almost impossible without assistance from an elaborate IT system to marshal and display enormous volumes of radar and other data. Radar will soon come into everyday use by motorists, and for those less-professional users microcomputers will manage the presentation of radar displays, and reduce the demands made on the driver's attention by providing vivid automatic warnings of potential collisions.

Safety when travelling is improved when IT is used to monitor the operation of engines and other vehicle components and controls. Microprocessors control the operation of aircraft engines in order to reduce noise and pollution, and to save fuel; and are now replacing hydraulic systems for operating the control surfaces. By their use the pilot is prevented from inadvertently initiating actions which would take the aircraft beyond its safe flying limits. The application of advanced automatic control and monitoring reaches its zenith when it is used to watch over the safety and economic operation of oil refineries, chemical plants and power stations. In these activities, an IT system is able to take a synoptic view of the whole operation, cope with immense flows of data, apply complex rules to the current situation and watch closely over the way it is changing in order to initiate rapid remedial action and keep an accurate and detailed log of events.

In some complex systems the appropriate corrective response can be counter-intuitive (that is surprisingly different from what unaided common sense would suggest) and is revealed only by the deep analysis of a mathematical model. IT enables us to make such analyses in 'real time' as things are developing in the system itself. This capability is invaluable, but it could tempt engineers to construct plants and systems that lie too far beyond the range of human comprehension and even beyond our ability to model with any assurance of accuracy or completeness. We should then have entered the terra incognita beyond the Bowden Limit[12], and 'here be dragons'.

Needless to say, it is vital to ensure that a single failure of the safety equipment or its programs must not be able to cause a dangerous mode of failure of the main plant. It is, therefore, usual to back the electronic safety system with conventional electrical or mechanical protectors, such as pressure-relief valves, and the use of IT should not be allowed to reduce the number of independent safety devices installed. Prudence also suggests that the IT system should incorporate means to test its own operation – the lifeboats must be launched from time to time and rowed around the ship.

Some complex systems lie at the limit of our understanding, and probably beyond our control. Yet we have to cope with them as best we may. One such is the weather. Accurate forecasts of impending gales, fogs, frosts or snow make for safer journeys, and have obvious economic value for farmers. Forecasting has been greatly improved by mathematical modelling of the atmosphere. The amount of calculation involved is heroic, and because it has to be completed before the weather arrives it stretches the power of the fastest computers. Meteorology and its allied subject aerodynamics are two of the few applications that are really limited by the power of available equipment. Systems operating an array of computers in parallel are well suited to handling atmospheric models. IT's other major contribution to weather forecasting is through the splendid images of cloud systems now provided by artificial satellites. With better data, improved understanding, and faster calculation it will soon be possible to extend the forecast period to several weeks, even for so uncertain a location as the British Isles.

Fast calculation has also advanced the science of structural design. Engineers are now able to complete the massive calculations their analyses require, and do so cheaply and in reasonable time. This allows them to explore a much larger variety of possibilities in order to select the best for a given application. They can check the strength and stability of their proposals, and investigate their modes of failure over a wide range of loadings and weather conditions. It is no longer necessary to multiply the dimensions of steelwork by so large a factor of safety – actually a factor of ignorance. That, however, introduces a risk that, emboldened by calculation, designers may cut the safety margins too finely in search of elegance or economy. Thus, a bridge that is strong enough to carry its intended load once erected may not be strong enough to withstand the higher stresses encountered during construction, and could collapse, causing a fatal accident while it is being built.

The use of IT encourages a hot pursuit of efficiency and economy, for this is the way it has been 'sold' to its users. Business generally is characterized by an ever-closer integration of activities which are not all necessarily owned and controlled by one company. Successful integration within a company, and externally with its suppliers, principal customers and bankers depends on copious and rapid exchanges of information. The result is efficiency, but the price is interdependence; for the tightly spun web of relationships is sensitive to disturbances in any of its parts, and to problems in the IT system itself. Not only does this underline the importance of integrity, reliability and security in that system, it also hands a greatly enhanced bargaining power to those who work with its computers and communications. Of course, as the system becomes more highly automatic the number of staff involved becomes fewer, but that gives even more power to the few who do remain. The more active trade unions, well aware of this development, are not averse to recruiting IT staff, who provide them with an effective lever for applying pressure to a recalcitrant employer. The effects are felt quickly, and because so few members are involved their action could be supported for ever by a modest levy on the rest.

Trades unions act in pursuit of the immediate microeconomic objectives of their members, but there are other pressure groups with less limited aims which range from international political factions to the purely crackpot. The small teams that design and operate IT systems could be infiltrated over a period in order to win a position from which costly disruption could be threatened unless some demand is met – a kind of data hijack. The fast-spreading use of IT cannot help but change the information infrastructure in ways that increase the vulnerability of an individual organization, and considerably enlarge the extent to which its paralysis would spread to affect interdependent activities. Hans Alfvén has painted a vivid scenario of such a breakdown[3]. We may need to consider carefully just how far we dare to go before our 'closely integrated' society becomes a dangerously 'highly strung' one.

Privacy

Of all the social changes that may be initiated by our use of IT, none has received more attention than the 'invasion of privacy', which it is feared may accompany the automatic processing of information. The subject came to life in 1966 in America when it was proposed to establish a National Data Center which would collect and collate information then being held piecemeal in the separate computer files of the Agencies and Bureaux of the U.S. government. In Britain, in 1987, there was a similar proposal to establish a Government Data Network to replace the couriers who carried data on magnetic tapes between departments. Because packet-switching would be used, it was claimed that only the hardware would be shared, and that each department would have its own 'virtual' network protected by software from indiscriminate or unauthorized access by others. That might even have been true, but software barriers are neither too difficult nor too costly to surmount should some future less-benevolent administration order a tighter integration.

In both the American and the British examples, the objectives were unexceptionable – to improve accuracy, efficiency and economy in the conduct of public business, rather than to increase surveillance of the citizen. However, as an American judge, Justice Louis D. Brandeis observed in 1928: 'Experience should teach us to be most on our guard to protect liberty when the Government's purposes are beneficent. . . . The greatest dangers to liberty lurk in insidious encroachment by men of zeal, well-meaning but without understanding'[13]. After a lengthy hearing before a Congressional Committee, the American proposal was shelved, but public discussion of the risks to the privacy of individuals exploded. This subject now has a longer bibliography, of lower quality, than any other connected with IT: the mere listing of publications on privacy would more than fill every page in this book. Special legislation has now been enacted in a number of countries[40], even at last in a reluctant Britain.

We need to be clear what is meant by 'privacy' when personal data are involved, and why IT is thought to pose a special threat. One dictionary defines privacy as 'being withdrawn from society or public interest; avoidance of publicity'. In these ordinary senses, most of the activities that disturb our privacy have nothing to do with IT. For instance: having our personal affairs reported in the press; being televised as a member of a crowd at a sports event; being photographed without our knowledge or consent by a remote or concealed camera; being overheard by a long-range microphone or electronic 'bug'; being quizzed for an opinion poll or market survey, or by traffic-survey officials; having unsolicited junk mail stuffed into our letter box.

In general, there has been no specific right to privacy, although respect for one another's privacy is widely regarded as a mark of civilized behaviour. In the context of IT, privacy refers to a person's right to control the supply and use of information about himself or herself. The personal data involved include: identifying characteristics; records of financial transactions; medical treatment; education; court records and so on: plus inferential data deduced from records of magazine subscriptions, attendance at meetings, membership of societies, and so forth. To be classified as personal, these data must be unambiguously associated with named individuals, or be capable of being traced to them.

Records of personal data have, of course, been kept for centuries before the advent of IT. Some administrative records of our interactions with government departments, with the courts and with commercial firms are more sensitive than others. And it has been the custom to hold those data in confidence unless and until they are required as legal evidence. Another class of personal records may be described as 'intelligence data', which are intended to help public authorities (for instance, the police and national security services) or private bodies (for example, providers of commercial credit) who in circumstances entirely relevant to their function need to be able to assess, predict or control the behaviour of a named individual. Such records are rarely published, indeed their very existence may not be acknowledged, and is not made known to those who feature in them.

Statistical and research records are in a different category, for the identity of a subject is detached before the record is processed. Again, data for several subjects may be grouped, or 'aggregated', which merges and to some extent conceals the identities of those concerned when the group is sufficiently large. Such data are unusually considered to be anonymous and to present little risk to privacy. However, statistics are collected to provide a factual basis for the formulation of government policies, and by highlighting 'abnormal' groups – teenagers say – some sections of the population may become statistical stereotypes, difficult cases requiring special treatment, and thus lose a kind of collective privacy.

IT is believed to present a new threat to personal privacy because of its efficiency in maintaining and processing vast files of information; as one American put it, 'it reduces the cost per unit of dirt dug'. It also makes it easy to collect and collate in one place information once held in various separate files. Moreover, those responsible for designing and operating IT systems are technical specialists who are not themselves interested in the use of data, and whose contacts with its users and providers are indirect: they tend to be concerned about efficiency and not at all about the social implications of what they are asked to do. There is no doubt that gathering together all the data about one person in one place does provide a much more effective instrument of understanding and control than when the same data are scattered over several files and file-keepers. The intelligence services have long known and used this kind of 'critical mass' effect.

For the most part, those using IT to record personal data are not entirely new organizations, they are the established bureaucracies of governments and private business. The worry about privacy is less about some novel threat and more about the fact that IT is enhancing the power of large corporations at the expense of individual freedom. In 1978, the British government maintained more than 250 different computer files that contained personal data[40]. These were by no means all equal in size or status; some contained only a few hundred entries, but the largest – the census records – had more than 74 millions. Personal records are also kept by health services, police forces, law courts, security services, education authorities, public utilities and local authorities. The list is a formidable one, and may suggest to the timid that Big Brother is about to arrive, admittedly somewhat later than 1984, but perhaps by 1994 – the doomsday date George Orwell would have chosen had he written his book one year later.

In a free and democratic society, few worry about the possibility of oppression or close surveillance by their elected government. Many accept that a government needs a great deal of personal information to administer with equity the complex web of legislation that directs and constrains its dealings with its citizens. If anything, governments have less information than they need to frame economic and social policies which are effective and relevant to contemporary problems and current needs. We face the *Catch 22* situation which dogs the early stages of all systematic studies – without information we cannot hope to achieve understanding, but without understanding we cannot determine what information we need. Fortunately, we do not have to solve all our problems at a stroke. We can hope to progress by that sequence of conjectures, refutations and refinement which has served us so well in the sciences.

A business requires IT systems to hold personnel records about its staff, and personal information about its suppliers and customers. Many of us use hire-purchase or some other form of credit, and 'credit reference agencies' exist by advising on our credit-worthiness. Most such agencies keep their records in computer files, and between them they hold information about many millions of us. These records contain rather sensitive personal information, and their occasional incompleteness and innaccuracies have sometimes resulted in a person being denied credit, or otherwise suffering in financial reputation. Banks, insurance companies, and building societies also hold records of our personal finances.

The booming use of credit cards means that we leave a trail as we encourage others to record our purchases of petrol, restaurant meals, hotel accommodation and so on. Organizations that use the post to sell goods or to collect subscriptions for clubs, magazines and charities keep records of our preferences to help them aim their mailshots more accurately; and in this way they construct revealing 'interest profiles' of their clients. These records are exchanged with other organizations, or sold to them; and their data are sometimes combined with information from published documents, such as an electoral register, to build up what amounts to a 'dossier' on an individual.

Privacy is the right of persons to determine how far, for what purposes, and with whom they are willing to share information about themselves, and six principles have emerged from the protracted debate on the subject.

(1) Individuals should be told of the existence of any file holding data about them, and should be able to examine their own records.

(2) Data must be obtained and processed lawfully, and when a request for statistical or research data is pick-a-backed on some routine return, it must be made clear which data the respondent is legally required to provide and which are being invited as a voluntary response.

(3) Personal data should be held for declared and lawful purposes only, and should be disclosed to no other user for any other purpose without the express written consent of the subject.

(4) Personal data must be accurate and kept up-to-date, appropriate to and adequate for the declared reason for holding it, but for no other; incorrect or obsolete data must be corrected and superfluous data erased.

(5) Personal data should be held for no longer than the period stated and agreed to be necessary when the purpose was declared and accepted.

(6) Adequate means of protection must be provided to prevent unauthorized access to personal data files.

The strict observance of these principles when designing and operating files containing personal data would do much to answer the doubts expressed about IT systems and privacy. Not that ordinary men and women are greatly bothered about these matters; those who protest are self-appointed defenders of civil liberties. Even they express alarm less about the possibilities of government tyranny than about the risks of embarrassing disclosures or unfair treatment. Less-advantaged sections of the public are more likely to worry about the fact that their circumstances may be inadequately recorded in government files, thus denying them social benefits to which they are entitled.

The sixth principle refers to protection; it is, of course, just as necessary to protect electronic files from prying eyes and fingers as it has been to protect four-drawer cabinets full of manilla folders. Unfortunately, security precautions codify and constrain the working conditions of those who operate IT systems, and quickly become irksome; they can also be expensive. A difficult balance has to be struck at which the level of security matches the expected risks of intrusion. It is necessary to recognize that if the procedures are too fussy the operators will inevitably scamp the tiresome rituals beloved of security consultants, or take a mischievous pleasure in skirting around them.

Since 1970, a number of countries have enacted laws to make failure to protect personal data a crime; and the ways used to protect IT systems are considered below under a more general discussion of computer crimes. The British government's approach to legislation was slow and unenthusiastic. Private members introduced Bills related to privacy in 1961, 1967, 1969 (2), 1970 and 1975, but none succeeded. The government stalled, and set up a committee which produced the Younger Report in 1972; that report was reviewed in two government White Papers in 1975. Those led to the establishment of yet another committee, which produced the final 460-page Lindop Report in December 1978[40].

Six years then passed before the Data Protection Act 1984 established a registrar whose duty it was to 'maintain a register of data users who hold, and persons carrying on computer bureaux who provide services in respect of, personal data'. The unregistered holding of personal data in computer systems was prohibited, and registered holders were required to observe principles similar to the six we listed above. Offenders can be de-registered and fined. The Act has been widely criticized as minimal and flawed. It does not apply to data held in official IT systems used to safeguard national security, nor to data about criminals held in police files, nor to files used to control tax evasion. It makes it an offence to disclose personal data to third parties, but very few IT systems have operating system software which logs each and every access to their records. So, how can anyone say who has had access over which data link to what data? And these times of instant and unrecorded communication via satellites will require a very much higher degree of international cooperation than has been usual if we are not to see 'data havens' spring up in countries whose laws are attractively relaxed.

The prolonged discussion of privacy has been emotive rather than rational; tongues wag, pens scratch and word-processor screens flicker, but minds rarely meet. The dangers foreseen are not confined to IT systems, but their high speed of processing, plus the ease with which enormous volumes of data can be collected and stored, means that we can now combine and collate information that would have previously remained disconnected and dispersed. As the Lindop Report noted: 'items of information which are harmless in isolation can become sensitive in combination'[(40)]. Moreover, with IT, storage and use do not have to take place in a single location, for a databank is a concept, not a particular machine; it does not have to be physically situated in one room; all the data stored in a distributed IT system can be regarded as existing simultaneously at every point in its network.

We fear what we do not understand, hence ordinary men and women fear IT more than they fear filing cabinets. To them, the consequences of using computers to keep personal records, and telecommunications to make them available worldwide, have introduced a new and significant social change, and one that needs control. And yet we must not overact by imposing restrictions which will frustrate or delay the beneficial social changes that ought to flow from improved information about the circumstances and needs of the population. Moreover, measures to protect privacy inevitably conflict with the demands for a free press and more open government; and the media argue powerfully and plangently for those two basic attributes of a democracy.

Crimes with and against IT

Crimes that involve IT combine two highly newsworthy topics, with the added spice that some human individual has defeated the mighty machine and embarrassed a powerful corporation. There is no need to recount here what has already received headline treatment. What we need to consider is how, if at all, the use of IT may change the nature and extent of criminal behaviour, whether by acts which injure the system itself or by crimes which exploit some application of it.

Crimes of the first kind are obviously a new social phenomenon, and so far have been relatively few in number. Disgruntled staff have sabotaged or maliciously damaged their employer's equipment, usually by setting fire to it, or even to the extent of shooting at it with a revolver, which does suggest extreme emotion. Apparently motiveless attempts have been made to bomb computer installations, and terrorists have bombed a few for ideological reasons. University students have attempted to destroy the magnetic tapes containing their academic records.

Specialist skills can be used to eavesdrop on the data messages flowing in an IT system. The blunt, brute force, method of attack is by 'wire tapping' in which a physical connection is made directly to one of the system's telecommunication channels. When these pass over a microwave or a satellite link, messages can be intercepted by a suitably positioned radio aerial and receiver. Weak electromagnetic radiations (radio waves) can also leak out of telecommunications equipment and from computer hardware; they can be picked up over distances of a few hundred metres by a simple aerial and receiver mounted in a vehicle. Signals garnered by whatever method are usually recorded for later analysis. When, however, they are those to and from a single remote terminal, and the system's standards are known, the criminal can use a similar terminal to display them, and may even be able to inject false messages to command or confuse the system.

Computer operators have been known to make deliberate mistakes to cause a system to crash, either as a revenge against the local management or to augment their own earnings by the overtime worked to recover the situation. It has also been alleged that dishonest programmers employed on short-term contracts have planted deliberate errors which are not immediately obvious, but which will ensure that they are recalled to do more work to remove them. Brian Randell has been heard to say that this is the sort of service provided by 'Trojan Horse Software Inc.' In a technique known as 'trapdoor and patch' an unscrupulous skilled programmer conceals a self-rewarding, or a destructive, sequence of instructions (the patch) beneath a 'trapdoor' inserted into an application program. Such a trapdoor consists of a conditional jump instruction that would be passed over unnoticed in normal use. Only when the criminal injects into the input data a pre-arranged code group that could not occur in the ordinary course, is the branching condition met, the trapdoor opened and the patch entered and obeyed. When the motive is purely destructive or the patch is to be obeyed only once, its last instructions would cause it to be erased to prevent subsequent discovery, for which reason it has been called a 'logic bomb'; when instead of an input code the trapdoor opens at a pre-set date and time it has been called a 'logic time bomb'. One accounting package sold for use by retail shops was found to contain a concealed patch which enabled the shopkeeper to hide part of his takings from the tax inspectors.

The trapdoor technique could also be used to insert an undetectably short sequence which has been designed to generate a much longer set of instructions which would then corrupt, erase or misplace filed data or confuse their processing. Such a sequence has been named a 'computer virus', for although very small and inconspicuous its malign effects could ramify throughout the affected computers terminals and links of an IT system. It is a technique with obvious appeal to an enemy agent or a terrorist, as well as to the merely mischievous or the criminal.

Computer programs have themselves become a valuable commodity, and an illicit but growing industry is producing pirated copies of commercial software, especially that aimed at the mass markets of personal and desktop computers. After a lot of debate about the nature of the property rights in software, it has been concluded that it is not an invention that can be patented, but should be brought under the laws of copyright. The British Copyright (Computer Software) Amendment Act 1985 extended the 1956 Act to cover software written in any programming language, but some problems remain. Thus, the Act is unclear about the modification of a program to allow it to be run under a different operating system. And when books or articles are produced with the help of a computer there are problems related to the degree of human skill involved, which obviously varies as between, say, the fully automated production of a telephone directory and the use of a word-processor when writing a novel. In America, the owners of copyright works are not obliged to show direct human involvement in order to establish their rights to protection.

It is also possible to misappropriate computer services. The operators or programmers may use the system without payment, or may sell its use to outsiders; and they may conceal their crime by entering data to mislead the programs that account for the use of the system, or alter the operations log to skip over periods of unauthorized activity. Programmers may use the system to develop software for private sale, to produce pirate copies or to perfect schemes for defrauding the system. Personal information of a potentially damaging kind could be copied and used for blackmail. Commercially confidential information, for example contract proposals and prices, or details of a new product design, could be stolen in an act of industrial espionage.

Most reported computer crimes, however, have concerned financial transactions, and have followed the well-trodden paths of fraud, theft and false accounting. The new features which IT introduces are speed and inconspicuousness, for the criminal act can be confined to a brief moment of illicit operation from a remote terminal, and the resulting action inside the system is still briefer and even less apparent. The opportunities are inevitably increased when the employee works from home. So far, the methods used have not been particularly subtle, nor have they required a deep expertise. For instance, a pay clerk has substituted his own pay number in other employee's data about overtime; the names of imaginary employees and of dead pensioners have also been used to enrich the criminal. Bank employees have diverted deposits to the account of a non-existent customer for subsequent collection. Some IT systems rounddown small amounts – British banks, for instance, did not deal in halfpence (now demonetarized), and instructions have been fraudulently inserted into accounting programs to divert the roundings into a fictitious account. This has been called the 'salami technique', for the criminal collects his loot in many very thin slices. Again, charges for goods and services have been inflated, and goods have been diverted by entering false delivery instructions.

The invention of nicknames, such as 'salami technique' and 'logic bomb', is often a sign that those concerned are seeking to mitigate their actions by making their moral lapse seem less heinous by implying that it is a general practice, or a mere prank, rather as small boys excuse their theft of apples from an orchard as 'scrumping'. There are other nicknames for computer frauds. 'Data diddling', which is probably the most common method and consists in changing one piece of data for another. 'Piggybacking' describes the practice of obtaining illicit entry to a system by riding on the back of a legitimate user, either by obtaining and using his password, or by following an authorized user through a locked door into a computer room by looking helpless with both hands full of magnetic tapes or discs. We have already referred to the trapdoor technique, which can provide undetected access to a program. The most dangerous of all methods has been called 'zapping'; in it an unscrupulous programmer obtains access to the privileged instructions or commands that afford direct links to the operating system itself. These are meant for use only in cases of malfunction, and any system is extremely vulnerable to criminal modification of its operating system; all programs and all files of data are then open to corruption.

One group with specialist knowledge and a nickname are the

'hackers'. Some of them are amateurs, but all are obsessed with the intellectual challenge of computing (Fig. 4). The growth of IT networks accessible over public telephone services has provided hackers with an irresistible target, and they are prepared to devote a great many hours to solving the fascinating puzzle of how to break into a commercial or governmental system. They are, indeed, the most common variety of attacker, and have been blamed for some criminal frauds. Clearly they have the opportunity, for there are plenty of insecure IT systems to tempt them, and they have developed programs to increase their own productivity by causing their personal computer to bombard a target system with a range of possible passwords at the rate of several hundreds a minute. Many hackers are teenagers whose motive seems to be mischievous pleasure at beating the adult world rather than criminal intent, and like noisy motorcyclists they are little more than a public nuisance. Hacking – obtaining unauthorized access to an IT system – is not itself a crime, but there are moves afoot to make it so.

Most of the crimes against IT systems result from someone's realization that there are exploitable weaknesses in their checking procedures. Few of them are specific to IT, and they tend to be the

Fig. 4. The hacker strikes again! (*Courtesy of Sam Smith.*)

same old crimes adapting themselves to a new electronic environment. But, what about the criminals? The evidence suggests that IT crime is a white-collar occupation for young men. Many of those who have been caught have been first offenders who were previously considered by their employers to be reliable, honest and intelligent. Their crimes have not involved personal violence, and they have injured a large machine system or an impersonal corporation rather than visible and vulnerable human beings. The offenders, therefore, tend not to be concerned about the moral aspects of their actions, and to worry only about the risk of exposure and the social injury that this would cause to their family and friends. Relatively few of those who have been detected have been IT specialists, but most have been connected in some way with the legitimate use of the system. IT crimes are usually insider jobs.

Some commentators, anxious to defend IT systems, suggest that they are in fact safer than manual ones, with proportionately fewer crimes, although the sums of money stolen on each occasion have been larger. This may not be the true picture for it seems that a number of cases which have been exposed by audit, or revealed by accident, have not been reported to the police; and that perhaps as few as 10% of discovered crimes have been pressed to public trial[4, 22]. A business which has suffered losses may prefer to absorb these rather than advertise the weakness of its financial controls, or destroy its customers' faith in an IT system which it would be very costly and very troublesome to alter or abandon.

The increasing use of IT in all our affairs, and the growing scope for crime, require us to take security precautions if we are to avoid adverse social consequences[68]. Broadly speaking, the measures available are of three kinds: physical, computer-based, and administrative.

IT installations must first be protected against natural hazards and human malice by keeping up-to-date copies of working programs and data files in a separate 'disaster store' located far enough away to be safe from any fire, flood, accident or attack that may affect the working installation. The risk of hostile human action can be reduced by exercising strict control over access to operational rooms, including the disaster store. Electronic locks, smart cards and intruder alarms have their parts to play; but so have cackling geese, fierce dogs and surly guards. 'Waste' of all kinds – paper, carbons and printer ribbons, magnetic tapes and floppy discs must be destroyed by thorough burning to prevent the illicit recovery of the information recorded upon them. Microcomputers are particularly vulnerable when they are situated in an insecure outer office; and some have been sent to be repaired with confidential information still recorded on their discs.

Because most IT crimes have been committed by trusted insiders, there must be a stringent control over the removal of magnetic tapes and discs and printed output, by anyone. Where the need for security is especially high, care will be taken to look for the use of electronic 'bugs', and metallic screening plus the installation of electrical filter circuits in the power cables will be used to contain the radiation of electromagnetic signals from the equipment and its communication links.

The design of an IT system should incorporate security measures from the start, for it is difficult, expensive and disruptive to graft them on later, and the result is rarely satisfactory. The aim should be to restrict or detect unauthorized access to programs and data. Thus, it makes good sense to segregate the programs and data files of different users, even though this reduces the advantages of a common database. It may be necessary to schedule separate periods for processing particularly sensitive work, and to purge the system of all programs and data before and after each period. It is especially important to ensure that programmers employed to modify working programs are closely supervised to make certain that no unauthorized change is made, and no trapdoor or patch inserted.

All messages from remote terminals must be checked to restrict the use of the system to authorized persons who are positively identified as operating the terminal they are cleared to use, for the purposes specified (and no other), and at the prescribed times of day. The current forms of identification are a password, or a coded magnetic card; more secure forms may in future depend on signature analysis, or on smart cards carrying biometric data such as voiceprints or retinal patterns. Or an essential part of the program may be recorded only on the smart cards of legitimate users. In too many systems the passwords chosen by users are naively easy to guess and, to be secure, passwords must be changed at frequent and unpredictable intervals. The patterns of operation of individual users from particular terminals, and their accessing of individual records and programs should be logged. Any significant change in use, such as an increased volume of messages to or from a given terminal, or a change in its times of use, or in the types of transactions initiated, are automatically noted and reported to the security controller – who should preferably have a suspicious mind, and an ulcer.

Messages to and from terminals, and possibly all data in files, can be encoded; but the encryption key must be changed often and randomly as a precaution against disclosure by a corrupt or compromised employee. The risks are, of course, greatest in systems which use public telecommunication services with one of the standardized arrangements for the exchange of data. Open systems interconnection and security are necessarily somewhat in conflict. Complicated problems can arise when two networks with different levels of protection are interconnected. Encryption and other protective techniques necessarily absorb some of the capacity from the computers and the communication channels of an IT system, and a balance has to be struck between security and efficiency. Often sheer speed of reaction is the best form of protection, for then by the time the 'opposition' has acquired your data it is too late for them to spoil what you want to do.

For maximum protection it must be quite impossible for a terminal user to seize control of the operating system software. This can be prevented by using separate software that can be accessed only from a privileged and well-guarded terminal; that software is then used to monitor and control all security measures. Alternatively, an entirely separate and independent supervisory computer can be used. It goes without saying that the person allowed to operate these core systems must be incorruptible, as must the engineers who maintain them.

Indeed, the most important contribution to security is to ensure that only reliable staff are engaged, for a dishonest employee with inside knowledge can frustrate any security system. The organization of work should respect the well-established principle of the 'separation of functions'. Regular audits and random security inspections are proven administrative methods for ensuring conformity with the rules, and delaying the onset of complacency. It can be a salutary, and a humbling, experience to commission independent experts to attempt to penetrate the system in order to reveal its weak points.

Security cannot be achieved without cost and effort. The costs include the salaries of security staff, purchase and installation costs for alarms, locks and so on. There are adverse effects on the attitudes and morale of the staff, for they will be chafed by identification procedures and access controls, and disturbed by the general atmosphere of suspicion. Finally, given time and a strong enough motive, a determined IT expert can penetrate the security of even the most elaborate system – the important thing is to see that sufficient time is not available. So far, however, high professional expertise has not been applied to IT crimes – or at any rate not to those unsuccessful ones that have been detected. The criminal's most satisfactory approach is still to corrupt and blackmail a key employee, and that is a method of operation they well understand.

Police work

IT may be adding appreciably to the amount of crime the police have to handle, but it is also being used by them in the fight against it. Police work requires a sensitive and delicate balance to be struck between the liberty of ordinary citizens and the close surveillance needed for the detection of crime and the arrest of suspects. The use of IT by the police could disturb the established balance and cause unwelcome social changes.

Our concern is not with the day-to-day management of a police force, for that closely resembles the management of any other organization of its size, but with the collection and use of the information – the criminal intelligence – on which success heavily depends. Because motorways enable criminals to travel far and fast, police information must be available nationally and immediately. In the computerized database of a police force it is useful to record information about known criminals, on missing and wanted persons, on stolen vehicles, on vehicle owners and on drivers' licences. Many other items could be of legitimate interest to the police, but these few suffice to show the difficulty of reconciling the liberty of the people with the efficiency of their police.

The recording of information about known criminals is necessary and socially acceptable provided 'criminal' and 'information' are each appropriately defined. Obviously, criminals are those who have been convicted of offences, but should there be a limit of time after which reformation, or at least retirement, can be presumed? Should minor offences, such as obstructing the police or shoplifting, be recorded? or semi-political ones, such as taking part in a rowdy demonstration? Such hard information as name, date of birth, sex and physical appearance is beyond reasonable objection, but what about more speculative material such as unproved criminal activity, or suspicious associates?

Lists of cars with their owners and drivers are clearly of great value, but they also allow the police to trace the movements of citizens who may be mistakenly suspected of involvement in a crime – say because their car was quite innocently parked in what became the vicinity of a crime, or was stolen or borrowed in suspicious circumstances. In Hong Kong, tests have been made of a system designed to reduce traffic congestion. Vehicles were fitted with electronic devices which generated identification signals whenever the vehicle passed over wire loops buried in the roadway. The signals were fed back to a central computer and used to levy selective tolls on individual users of city-centre streets. Similar trials in the USA were made with the different object of tracing the movements of stolen vehicles, heavy trucks in particular. The trucks were inconspicuously weighed at the same time to check for illegal overloading. Each of these systems offers the police the opportunity for close surveillance of all vehicles and journeys, including those of private citizens going about their social and business affairs. So potent a facility is open to abuse, and would need to be subject to careful control under the authority of the courts. It would, moreover, bear most harshly on ordinary men and women, for criminals of every kind would quickly learn the art of tampering with the electronic identifiers, and add that to the list of computer crimes.

There can be no doubt that IT is increasing the efficiency of police record-keeping and removing constraints on the accessibility and volume of recorded material; but that is not itself the prime reason for concern. Our attitude to police records essentially reflects our attitude to the police themselves. If we believe that they can and should be trusted, then our fears will be minimal. Because this is obviously a desirable state of affairs, our concern should be to encourage them – with external advice and under lay supervision – to operate with an acute and evident sense of social responsibility. Of course, happy acceptance of that view will come less readily to members of minority groups which the majority find odd or disturbing – anarchists or drug users, for example. But it would be unfair to blame the police for reflecting the general public attitude. If we dislike or distrust police methods we must strive to reform them; it would be stupid to deny them the help of IT in fighting crime.

IT and war

The day-to-day control of an army, navy or air force is very much like the management of any other large organization, and the use of IT for housekeeping purposes raises no special problems beyond those raised by similar applications in business and industry. Indeed, to the extent that IT makes defence forces more efficient and economical it should free resources for uses of more immediate benefit to men, women and society. The potentially disturbing changes are those related to the use of IT in weapons and for military intelligence.

IT systems can be programmed to act, both locally and remotely, as very effective automatic controllers; indeed, without their aid it would not be feasible to use most current weapons[6]. Those of us who fear nuclear war should blame silicon as much as uranium or plutonium; they make the bang, but silicon determines precisely where the bang will occur. Consider, for example, a rocket designed to intercept and destroy enemy missiles. A warning that missiles appear to have been launched and a plot of their course will be given and continuously updated by long-range radars, airborne as well as ground-based. These use computers to process their radio signals in order to disentangle echoes generated by an enemy attack from the confusing background of radio noise and interference, and from decoy and masking signals emitted by the enemy. The results are fed into an IT system that combines data from many sources, including satellite and other intelligence reports, in order to maximize the information presented to the defence commander. He or she then has to decide whether to initiate a counter attack and designate its initial targets. Once that has been done, ground computers will calculate the flight paths for the intercepting missiles, aim them at pre-determined targets, and fire them at appropriate times. Continuous control will be maintained in flight by air-borne microcomputers on each missile, and the ground-based IT system will check their flights and abort the attack if circumstances change.

The speed of delivery of rocket-propelled missiles and the fact that their use cannot be confirmed until they have been launched, means that a defence commander has very little time in which to decide whether and how to respond. The awesome destructive power of nuclear warheads greatly increases the 'advantage' of making the first strike by a surprise attack, and that requires defence forces to remain on perpetual alert – not an easy condition to sustain during a long period of peace. The intensive use of IT in defence systems is designed both to accelerate the speed of response by 'taking the man out of the control loop' and to maintain a fully alert state immune to fatigue, boredom or distraction.

Counter-attack is well established as an effective method of defence, but no one has yet proposed to automate the final decision to retaliate. That dreadful decision remains with the head of government, who would be forced to take it with uncharacteristic speed and resolution. He or she would be advised by senior military staff and by political colleagues, who would themselves be advised by their experts, who would in turn rely on the promptings of their 'expert knowledge-based' IT systems. The speed and complexity of a major nuclear attack leaves no other option. Let us hope that those experts, and the IT system designers, have sufficient humility to recall Oliver Cromwell's warning 'to consider that you may be mistaken'. The scenarios they have built in and programmed are a massive commitment of thinking and spending, but they could be misconceived. Flexibility is at least as necessary as pre-conceived responses, however effective those might be in the assumed circumstances; for an enemy will hope to be able to act or react in ways that we have not foreseen and anticipated. The head of government's first decision is whether and how far to trust the experts: that problem we shall take up in a wider context in the next chapter.

Obviously, when IT systems are used in so crucial a role as defence decisions, malfunctions and errors must be minimized – elimination is impossible. Silicon-chip hardware is extremely reliable both for computing and for communications; it can also be triplicated and its results accepted only when all three systems agree. Software errors are less easy to handle. Triplication can help with errors of copying, or those occurring randomly within the hardware, but it can do nothing about errors of conception or of logic made by the programmers. Moreover, the programs needed for defence data analysis and weapon control are necessarily long and elaborate, and the number of alternative routes through them is so astronomically large that it is not feasible to demonstrate by operational tests that no error remains. The quiddities of real life and the laws of Murphy combine to preclude any such happy result. Clearly, operational trials are invaluable as a way of combing out the grosser errors, but undetected errors almost certainly lurk in obscure corners within all major programs. Unfortunately, no one has been able to devise formal analytical methods of proof which can be used for programs of significant length. We cannot, therefore, remove completely the risk that a few subtle errors remain in defence-system software – 'theirs' as well as 'ours'. War always involves the acceptance of risks, and they could even be fewer when IT is used, but we must not be so carried away by technological enthusiasm as to take every last man 'out of the control loop'. IT can be used to take the strain, but not the blame.

On a conventional battlefield, individual soldiers are being equipped with 'smart' weapons for use against enemy tanks and aircraft. These are rocket-propelled bombs which can be launched bazooka-fashion from a portable firing tube, and guided by an infrared laser towards the chosen target, which they will identify in broad terms by using an on-board microcomputer to analyse the target's image and compare it with a stored proto- type. Once launched, such a missile needs no further attention from the soldier; it is a 'fire and forget' device, and one that can carry several warheads travelling independently to confuse a counter-attack.

The extensive use of IT in war and defence has stimulated the growth of a derivative and substantial industry devoted to 'elec- tronic warfare'. One part of this activity seeks to discover what signals a potential enemy is using, and for what purposes; it does so by scanning the radio spectrum automatically and system- atically to reveal which wavebands and what kind of signals are being used. When these facts are established, electronic counter- measures can be devised to disrupt enemy systems. This can be achieved crudely and bluntly by generating powerful jamming emissions, for example to mask the weak radar echoes that could reveal our own dispositions. More subtly, we can send decoy signals to confuse or mislead the enemy's equipment and divert the attack to harmless targets.

We must assume that an enemy will be using kinds of elec- tronic surveillance and counter-measures similar to our own, and another branch of electronic warfare deploys various techniques designed to protect our military services. Thus, radar and field communications will not use just one radio-frequency channel but will hop between a number of alternatives: the hops occur many times a minute in a sequence that is prearranged but unpredictable. Alternatively, the message may be divided be- tween several channels operating simultaneously; in the 'spread spectrum' technique the signals are smeared out to resemble radio noise. Communication signals may also be bunched very tightly together and squirted out in brief high-speed bursts at irregular intervals. Civilian radar and communications signals consist of trains of short pulses at precisely regular intervals; in their military equivalents the repetition of pulses is 'jittered', (that is, varied abruptly, frequently and randomly) in order to add to the difficulties of unfriendly analysis.

Aircraft and missiles carry receivers to detect the arrival of enemy radar or jamming signals. The response may be to disperse a cloud of 'chaff' – strips of metal foil which are left behind or shot off sideways to produce stronger radar echoes than the hoped-for target. Some missiles may even be programmed to home-in on and destroy the sources of whatever enemy signals they detect. Military aircraft are being designed to reduce their propensity to reflect radar signals. The techniques have attracted the generic name 'stealth', and include the elimination of abrupt projections and sharp corners; attempts are also being made to devise surface coatings with a low reflectivity for radio waves – their optical equivalent would be dull black.

Military communications traditionally use ciphers, and it has become known that the first electronic computers to be used operationally were the Colossus machines constructed at the British Post Office Research Station during the 1939–45 war to help in breaking the German Enigma codes. The subsequent development of IT enables very elaborate codes to be used entirely automatically. We assume, however, that any code can be broken by sufficient computing power; the aim is to require so much time and effort that the decoded result will not become available until it is too late to help an enemy, and also to change the code at intervals which are significantly shorter than the likely decryption time. Battlefield communications may be sent in clear rather than using elaborate ciphers, relying instead on speed of action to frustrate any effective enemy response.

Nuclear explosions generate a very brief, very intense, surge of electromagnetic waves known as an electromagnetic pulse, or EMP, which induces powerful electric currents in metallic objects. Electronic equipment can be put out of action by these currents, and military electronics need to be protected (hardened) against EMPs by heavy metallic shields. Optical fibres and switches are relatively immune to the nuclear EMP, which lends impetus to the development of all-optical IT systems; they are, of course, vulnerable to the cruder mechanical and thermal assaults of an explosion.

The Duke of Wellington once said: 'all the business of war . . . is to endeavour to find out what you don't know by what you do'. A simple but effective way to obtain information about the capabilities and intentions of a potential enemy is to accumulate and analyse every scrap of information that comes to hand. Some of this will come from openly published material, some from espionage, some from reconnaissance by satellite and radar, and some from electronic surveillance which intercepts signals leaking out of the enemy's territory and from operations overseas, and indeed underseas. The great capacity of an IT system for acquiring, storing and collating separate items of data – the very features which give rise to our fears about personal privacy – help considerably in intelligence work. It is difficult to decide whether a general improvement in military intelligence would advance or retard the cause of peace. A major problem is that international events and policies are influenced more by the perceptions of national governments than by the facts. Moreover, as we noted earlier (Chapter 3), facts are not absolute truths waiting passively somewhere out there for us to discover them. We fish for data in the turbulent stream of events, and those we happen to catch we interpret by criteria of relevance that we believe to fit our immediate purpose. What is certain, however, is that the advent and enthusiastic adoption of IT by the military, and the economic momentum acquired by the defence electronics industry, have transformed the situation and will continue to do so.

A long time ago, British officer cadets were trained in command by TEWTS (tactical exercises without troops), using toy soldiers and sand trays. It has long been the aim of commanders to determine the enemy's plans in order to know which strategy will succeed and which will not, to agitate him and ascertain the pattern of his movements; to probe him and learn. It is no longer considered necessary to agitate and probe an actual enemy in the field. In today's high speed wars it would be too late anyway; and in today's fragile peace it would be too risky. It is now possible to

provide convincing simulations of battle manoeuvres and possible enemy reactions by using IT equipment programmed to drive
displays. This sort of electronic war game can be enlarged in
scope and increased in complexity almost without limit in order
to provide models of full-scale wars in which a nation may be
involved with a range of possible enemies, and in association
with a variety of assorted allies. To the extent that such simulations can be made realistic enough to serve the purposes of
strategic analysis, they ought to help to ensure that the military
advice given to governments will be more soundly based. We can
welcome changes in that direction, for they seem likely to discourage heedless adventurism; although the blind ferocity of
fanaticism and the corrupting lure of instant political gains are
not easy to quantify, and foolish to discount. Fortunately, any
stabilizing influence is most likely to be effective in those nations
which are most advanced in their use of IT, for they happen also
(and it is no coincidence) to be those whose weapons have the
greatest potential for causing human misery. But we really must
remember GIGO (garbage in, garbage out), and to that healthy
precept let us add CLOD (conception limited, output dubious).
Whether or not artificial intelligence is ever realized, IT certainly
acts as an amplifier of human intelligence, but amplifiers magnify
rather than improve, and IT may merely make the failings of our
analyses larger and more troublesome. There is no reason to
suppose that the military modelling of tactical and strategic situations is exempt from the problems that afflict other kinds of
modelling, which we noted above (see Chapter 3).

Spending on defence is a large item in the budgets of the
technologically advanced countries: it is an even larger fraction of
the money which their governments allocate to research and
development. Some argue that this starves non-military work
and distorts the research programmes of businesses and universities; a few would even argue that it 'corrupts' the researchers
themselves. That we may doubt, for most young people focus
sharply and narrowly on the technical problem before them, and
worry far too little about the wider import. The standard reply to
such criticism is that the military requirement to develop

equipment and systems of high performance which are easy to use and reliable under hostile and distracting conditions has a stimulating effect on high-technology industry generally. Thus, the seeds of IT – pulse communications, radar, electronic computers – were sown in military research establishments during the last war. Few civilians need inter-continental missiles, but the rockets that propel them are also available to launch a communications satellite or an X-ray telescope. The science that underpins the explosive force of a nuclear warhead can also be used to enhance the efficiency and the safety of a nuclear power station. The detailed surveys of the seabed made for submarine warfare have added greatly to our geological knowledge, and have revealed resources that are exposing a new area for economic conflict between nations. This is the so-called 'spin-off' argument, which claims uncovenanted benefits from military research: common sense suggests that the same or greater benefits could be obtained by a direct approach which specificially pursues civilian ends. Certainly we could do that, but would we? Would we be willing to make massive public funds available to drive work ahead that might heap commercial advantages on a few? Education, medicine and many other social aims have skilful and persuasive advocates to urge their prior, and more ethical, claims on the public purse.

History suggests that agreed and urgent national aims are needed to mobilize and direct our resources. We lack such an aim in Britain. In America, space projects have long provided a surrogate war, although the race to put a man on the moon had obvious military overtones as well as those of national pride. It has, indeed, been the insatiable demands of space and defence, backed by the long purse of the Pentagon and the lobbying of the electronic industries, which have fuelled the development of microelectronics and IT, and have driven them ahead so fast that, as a side-effect, we face the social changes that so concern us today.

Without question, the military use of IT has changed the threat of war and undermined the security of ordinary men and women, and it is only the smallest consolation to know that the increasing accuracy claimed for missile guidance systems means that civilian targets are less likely to be hit unintentionally. Precise targetting could mean that specific cities are more likely to be used as 'hostages' to be threatened at will in the ploys which make up the labyrinthine games of international arms negotiation. Today's complex offensive and defensive weapon systems rely totally on IT and could not operate without it. In that way, at least, IT has changed the relations and the tensions between the major powers, and not only has altered the actual risks of war but also has had differential effects on governments' perceptions of those risks. It is only fair to point out that the development of methods of seismic analysis for geological surveying has provided a way of monitoring the observance of a 'test ban treaty' for nuclear weapons.

A well-established tactic in commercial competition is to set a crippling pace of innovation in the hope of 'burning off' the opposition. It has frequently been used in IT where, by a fortunate quirk, it has not always favoured the rich and the powerful. Small firms, untramelled by the bureaucracy that is irresistibly attracted to large organizations, have been able to outpace more formal giants. On the international scene, fierce innovation in the warlike applications of IT may now be being used consciously and deliberately as an arm of economic warfare in which potential adversaries attempt to force each other into a disruptive diversion of public programmes and resources in a futile and illusory attempt to secure enduring military superiority. If we can learn anything from military history it should be that the race between the weapon-smith and the armourer is everlasting and unwinnable. This is more than ever true when innovation is as rapid as it has been with IT. By the time a new system can be manufactured and troops trained in its use, it will have been made obsolete at least once by the next development; but that, unfortunately, could persuade its owners to use it before it is hopelessly outclassed.

Postscript

It is not feasible to cover all of the ways in which IT is already bearing on our affairs; new applications appear every day. Its unremitting permeation of our lives is not the result of some master plan, but is happening piecemeal as suppliers sell and users install systems in the pursuit of their own immediate and particular purposes. And yet, what we are seeing is more than creeping modernization, for IT does not merely mechanize and motorize, it roots out the old and sows anew. In small applications this radical replacement need cause us no alarm, for the effects of success are moderate and those of failure are limited. But, for the more massive systems now being developed, two facts should make us pause.

The first is that no one yet knows how to prove absolutely by logical analysis that their programs are free from error, and it is not practicable to test them exhaustively. For critical applications it is not enough to demonstrate that certain items of input data produce the expected results; to be assured adequately we need to check and approve the processes which generated those results. Most IT systems are designed to respond to data and commands whenever these happen to arise, interrupting whatever they were working on at the time; and it is particularly difficult to assess or to test the full range of interactions that can develop between successive or clashing interrupts. Usually the consequences of program errors are obvious and limited, recovery is easy, and the penalty is little more than annoyance followed by modest compensation. However, the consequences of software errors in the systems used to guide or to intercept nuclear missiles are much more alarming, and it is the practical impossibility of testing large interconnected systems which has caused a number of IT specialists to criticize, and some to withdraw from, work on the American 'Star Wars' defence initiative.

The second cause for concern is that it is never possible to do just one thing. The launch of a ship creates waves that can swamp a nearby quay. The commissioning of a major IT system inevitably disturbs many more than the few who paid for it to be installed. Those who design large systems are rarely encouraged to consider what waves its operation may generate. Nor, are they given the time or the resources to adjust their designs to minimize the radiating effects that may be caused.

Attempts are being made to set standards that will enable IT systems to communicate more freely with each other over common networks. The aim of this 'open systems interconnection' is the increased efficiency and economy which is to be achieved when manufacturers, wholesalers, retailers, customers, banks and government departments communicate rapidly and automatically. Integration is the name of the game: internal integration between the departments within a firm; external integration between it and all its business correspondents. In the limit, businesses and governments would be linked to form a supersystem of more than national scale; but unless specific measures are taken to prevent it, an unwanted disturbance in one part could propagate instantly, silently, and subtly to affect other distant systems. There is, however, no overall planning of even one country's network, nor outside of the centralized socialist economies is any likely: nor, indeed, can we be certain that anyone would be competent to do it. The most we can hope for is that designers will take care to ensure that their own systems are not so tightly coupled to others that they become dangerously vulnerable to those others' weaknesses and failures. I believe that this precaution is too important to be left to chance.

Privacy, computer crimes and police surveillance will each contribute headlines on slow news days. They do, nevertheless, present real risks which we neglect at our peril, but they grow from roots deeper and older than any new technology. Invasions of privacy, crimes and abuses of police powers would not vanish if IT were to be abolished, nor did they begin with its introduction. Even so, worries about them are not confined to lay people. Many IT specialists know that injury can arise as well from incompetence or carelessness as from dishonesty, and are concerned to raise the levels of competence, execution and ethics in their new profession. As an agent of social change, IT accelerates what has already begun and would have happened anyway; it has acted as a catalyst rather than a primary cause of change. It would be a grave error to allow our genuine worries about its effects to deflect our attention from more obdurate and obscure influences which are shifting the locus of power in our societies.

Any discussion of war and peace is brought face-to-face with nuclear weapons. For the most part, that large subject lies beyond our present brief; but on a narrow point they do, in their own macabre way, illustrate the diminishing returns of advancing technology of all kinds. Thus, one reason for applying IT to nuclear war has been to improve the accuracy of aiming long-range missiles. The distance that one is likely to land off-target has been reduced from 300–500 m to 100–200 m. Work is in hand to bring this error down to 10–20 m, and no doubt attempts will be made to cut it still further. As, however, the destruction and death caused by the explosion of their awful warheads extends to some thousands of metres, there is less and less point in positioning the centre of damage within ±10 m rather than ±100 m, or ±1 m rather than ±10 m. There can be little doubt that excellent minds will be bent to these objectives, or that they will be supported at immense cost to the public purse. Too often we immerse ourselves in the means and forget the ends: improving the instruments, polishing the tools, can be fascinating and challenging, but is essentially a subordinate, activity. The best way to avoid this misdirection of effort is, of course, to eliminate the risk of war, but governments have long found it convenient to raise the cry 'The enemy is at the gates' when they wish to divert our attention from their little local difficulties.

8
Matters of politics

Politics is about power, information is an instrument of power and IT has given us the most effective information systems we have ever had. But they are not equally available to all, and could shift the locus of political power yet further away from ordinary citizens. 'Democracy' is a word with many different meanings: until this century it was often a term of abuse, meaning 'mob rule'. Today, it is widely appropriated as a mark of approval – or of self-justification. I shall be using it in the restricted sense of 'representative democracy', and more particularly to denote the forms and styles of government current in Britain, in the USA, and in some other Western countries.

The will of the people

Representative democracy requires the consent of the governed, as expressed in the occasional election of representatives to local and national assemblies. Great emphasis is laid on this right to vote and on successive enlargements of the franchise to include women, those young enough for military service and the poor. Politicians congratulate themselves on giving so many of us the opportunity to participate in our own governing. Certainly we are able to make our views known to them by refusing to re-elect; but that method of protest has the defect of being sporadic, infrequent and less-rewarding than you had hoped.

Technically minded enthusiasts have proposed to use IT to speed up the electoral process, or even to supplement or replace it with frequent referendums conducted electronically. However, the essence of democracy is not to be found in the kitchen arrangements for determining the will of the majority, but in that majority's respect for the rights of all. The elected British assembly has been known to call itself the 'Mother of Parliaments', and the word 'parliament' derives from the verb 'to talk', not from the verb 'to vote'. An essential part of parliament's function is the pragmatic accommodation of the proposals of the majority to the views and rights of minorities. A change from marking ballot papers, or filing into voting lobbies, to pressing buttons would be an insignificant and gimmicky modernization.

Electronic referendums

A similar naive enthusiasm prompts even some politicians (when in opposition) to suggest using IT terminals associated with television receivers, or installed in public buildings, to provide a rapid, automatically totalled, voting system. Local and national referendums could then be used to 'bring decision-making closer to the people' by enabling the entire population to participate in deciding major policy questions – as in the Athenian 'cradle of democracy'. Parliaments, congresses and other assemblies would meet to work out the details of implementation.

Electronic referendums present no insuperable technical problem, but they do raise a number of non-technical questions. Many of today's political issues are complex and highly technical, and they would have to be butchered into a deceptive simplicity to provide a simple choice between a few crisp possibilities. Few men and women have the capacity to analyse these matters in depth, and fewer still have the inclination to devote the time and effort required to reach informed and reasoned conclusions. It is well known that answers can be steered by the way a question is phrased. Moreover, those answers may well be impulsive, emotional, responses rather than well-considered judgments, especially on such matters as abortion or capital punishment.

The media of public information and advertising are staffed by professionally skilled manipulators of public opinion. There can be little doubt that if electronic referendums were to become the rule, then the formidable apparatus of this mass-persuasion industry would be deployed by interested factions. A popular vote might then reflect little more than the performance of the most recent, most plausible, demagogue to appear on television, or the views of the party able and willing to spend most money. Clever and unscrupulous political leaders could easily massage the question and exploit the media to secure whatever answer was required to 'authenticate' their government's actions or intentions.

A change from good old-fashioned democracy to new-fangled electronic populism would be a sad decline from rational and responsible choice in our political affairs: and, once the novelty had worn off, it would probably bore the population to tears. Hans Alfvén has presented a witty and perceptive account of life controlled by electronic referendums[3]. In his *Complete Freedom Democracy*, the government ranks policy options by computerized cost-benefit analyses. Being obtusely rational, it always puts forward the best as its own proposal no. 1, but it also puts it, with the next-ranked as no. 2, no. 3 and so on, to all citizens for decision. Most citizens find incessant demands for personal votes a wearisome inconvenience, and fit their terminals with a device that silences the calling bell and automatically votes for proposal no. 1.

Pressure groups and single-issue politics

Electronic referendums would imprison political choice and force it to be exercised as starkly simplistic selections between specified alternative answers to stated questions. Public attention would be narrowly focussed on individual issues, rather than spread across a wider spectrum of political philosophies and programmes. One consequence would be to tip the balance of power away from political parties and towards single-issue pressure groups[57]. Special-interest groups organized to apply pressure for changes in law or custom are a feature of political life in this century. To their members they offer commitment to a clearly defined and coherent end, as opposed to the muddling compromises and serious misgivings associated with swallowing whole the policies of a party. They provide camaraderie and a sense of participation, plus the prospect of actually achieving some concrete result, which few men or women can hope to experience in ordinary political life. They do so by fragmenting the business of government into isolated issues, which they pursue vigorously but with little perception of, and no accommodation to, what may be best in the common good. Compromise in the broader interest is anathema; they thrive on single-minded conflict.

Pressure groups cannot claim to represent the views of a majority of the electorate. Typically, they are led by a few highly committed, highly articulate, middle-class activists. Their members are self-selected. Their views are not necessarily those of the apathetic mass of the population – certainly, they are not known to be so, nor does that seem to be a matter of concern to their leaders. Nature conservation is a popular cause in Britain, and few would dare to speak against it; but only about one person in 20 of the population belongs to a conservation society. Pressure groups are not limited to those with high-minded ethical aims. Chambers of Commerce, agricultural and industrial associations, trades unions and professional bodies all act as pressure groups to advance their members interests on agenda that are broader than a single issue, but narrower than those of the political parties. The sheer volume of governmental business requires an increasing number of important decisions to be delegated by representative assemblies to ministers and their civil servants. These are, naturally, lobbied by groups who win a hearing by interlarding their pleas with valuable specialist advice. Effective groups are also invaluable to the media as ever-ready sources of news and controversy. By lobbying, and through publicity, a pressure group can exert a political influence out of all proportion to its membership.

Were electronic referendums to become the norm, we could see a shift from the hierarchical order of government by representatives and assemblies towards the matrix organization currently in favour with management theorists. We would then have changed, probably insensibly and unwittingly, from government by elected generalists to policy determination by self-appointed specialists. And, that would raise the kind of questions about the effect of IT on the role of experts in government which are considered later in this chapter.

Opinion polls

Almost certainly, full-scale electronic referendums will remain no more than a technologist's fantasy, for elected politicians are most unlikely to hand over their hard-won power base to others. They have a more ambivalent attitude towards the mini-referendums now being conducted by commercial companies whose business it is to assess the views of the public by interviewing samples of the population. Originally developed for market research, opinion polling has found favour with the media as a convenient substitute for news. Political leaders affect a lofty disdain for poll results when these are unfavourable to them, but are less dismissive of any that flatter their chances.

The use of IT is not essential, although it has been used by television stations to collect instant phone-in answers to questions about a televised debate or presentation. The commercial polls invariably use computers to accelerate their analyses, and it is not seen as a disadvantage that computer processing lends an air of scientific objectivity and authority to their results. The accuracy and significance of those results depend on many factors: the number of persons interviewed; how truly representative a sample they were; their familiarity with the subject matter; the exact wording of the questions used; respondents' feelings about being invited to take part; their attitude to those asking the questions; and how settled and responsible, or how casual and volatile, are the views they express. Great accuracy is not to be expected. Official enquiries sometimes select names at random from electoral rolls, but it may then be necessary to make repeated visits to contact shift workers or those on holiday, and that makes this kind of sampling slow and expensive. The quick and dirty polls favoured by the media use 'quota sampling' in which the field workers are instructed to interview not named individuals but stated numbers of persons in each of several categories defined by age, sex, social class, economic activity and so on. Quota sampling is less accurate than a truly random sample, and when 1000 persons are interviewed the error is about ±4% at the 95% confidence level. That is, 95% of polls will give results within ±4% of the true value – one poll in 20 might have a larger error.

Enlarging the sample reduces the error, which falls to ± 3.4% when 1500 respondents are interviewed. Unfortunately, the accuracy improves only according to a square-root law, and to reduce the error to ± 1% the size of the sample, and so the cost of the poll, would need to be increased 10 times or more. Even so, the published results of polls are commonly stated to the nearest 1%. Their probable errors actually mean that although support for party A may be presented as 39%, giving it an apparent lead of 8% over party B at 31%, the real result for a sample of 1000 is A = 35 to 43%, B = 27 to 35%, which implies that A's lead over B lies somewhere between 0 and 16%, a much less newsworthy conclusion. Again, at best, polls reflect current opinions and cannot claim to predict how even those interviewed will actually vote at the next election. These pedantic objections in no way inhibit the media's use of poll results, or the jittery reactions of the financial markets to them. In the run-up to the British general election of 1987 the opinion poll results published almost every day by the media showed variations in support for the three principal parties as: Conservative 40 to 45%; Labour 28 to 37%; Alliance 18 to 26%. The election result was: Conservative 43%; Labour 32%; Alliance 23%.

It has been suggested that opinion polling could have various undesirable political consequences. Undecided voters who would like to feel that they are on the winning side may leap on to a bandwaggon. Conversely, those anxious not to 'waste' their votes may desert a predicted loser. Should the polls suggest that a party will win by a handsome margin, its lazier or more apathetic supporters may not take the trouble to vote. Timid electors may 'back-pedal' and refrain from voting for a party expected to win easily in order to preserve it from the arrogance that goes with having too dominant a majority in the assembly. 'Tactical voting' may take place where there is more than one opposition party; votes are then cast to defeat rather than to elect, and opponents who usually support party C switch their votes to party B in the hope of defeating the even more disliked party A. Tactical voting is not likely to be effective without the knowledge of party positions revealed by opinion polls.

It was widely believed that the frequent publication of poll results brought forward the date of the British election of 1987; and the prospects of a coalition seem to have affected the expectations of financial markets, and thus the actions of ministers. IT's combination of televised debates and interviews with opinion polling has also emphasized the influence of the public 'images' of parties and politicians. An experienced British parliamentarian, Michael Foot, has deplored the exaltation of the 'politics of perception' over the 'politics of persuasion', but today persuasion is more commonly achieved by image building than by rational argument.

Party workers and political journalists impatient to know the result before the votes have been counted may conduct 'exit polls' by asking electors how they cast their votes as they leave the polling stations. Even allowing for those awkward citizens who still believe in a secret ballot, an exit poll is likely to be reasonably accurate for it records a recent act rather than a future intention. Time-zone differences across the USA enable an exit poll to be completed on the east coast and its results broadcast while voters are still going to the polling stations in the far west. The publication of exit poll results has therefore been banned until after the last stations are closed, to avoid disturbing the democratic process. In Britain's 1987 election, the results of exit polls were not released on election day until after the financial markets had closed for business. For similar reasons it has been suggested that opinion polls should be banned in the period immediately before an election. It would certainly save a great deal of dreary speculation.

Packaged politics

The demon that tempts politicians to proclaim that they know what the people want – or even worse, 'what they really want', has persuaded some of them to employ market-research organizations to underpin their guesses. American political parties particularly, have spent huge sums on studies of data collected by telephone and cable television [56,51]. Their aim has been to identify what the public likes, and more importantly what it dislikes about their policies and their personalities. And, because bringing down an opponent is no less necessary, the perceived strengths and weaknesses of competing candidates are exhaustively analysed. Data have been collected for more than a hundred subgroups of the American electorate classified by age, sex, ethnic origin, religion, economic class, location and so on. Elaborate models have been constructed to answer those 'what-if' questions that advance the development of election strategies. The resemblance to war gaming is not accidental. The results can be applied to adjust the emphases and priorities placed on items of a party's programme, and to disguise blemishes on the public faces of its principals.

None of these cosmetic manoeuvres is cheap, which must raise questions of equity. Even more disturbing is the shift in power towards the pollsters as they set the political agenda and remodel the candidates. The result could be a shopping basket of policies specifically designed for maximum electoral appeal. That may appear to be a most democratic way of responding to the declared wishes of the people but, even setting aside the fallibility of poll results, it could decline into a slick sales campaign for oven-ready packages of currently popular nostrums rather than a coherent and responsible programme of legislation. Were that to happen, we the electors would cease to be the ultimate political masters and become pliant consumers of our government's goods and services. Who can doubt that our prejudices and our impulses would then be manipulated by means of Vance Packard's 'hidden persuaders', which are used with such deadly effect in retail selling[53].

When an election takes place, IT is used to increase the efficiency of canvassing. Party workers classify the list of electors in their constituency by age, sex, ethnic group, occupation, economic class, house and share ownership, mail-order purchases, subscriptions to magazines and to charities, religion, canvassing and voting records from previous elections where known, and so on. Door-to-door visiting, campaign literature, and messages sent over cable television channels can then each be tailored selectively to achieve the maximum effect on individual electors.

The unpleasing practices of telephone selling may be used, and computer control enables numbers to be dialled automatically and pre-recorded exhortations poured into the ears of those unwary enough to listen. None of this is novel, it is a simple extension of previous practice; but the availability of microcomputers and packaged programs has made election IT very cheap.

Big brother

George Orwell's date may have passed but his nightmarish vision of dictatorship remains. Certainly, IT could be used by an oppressive government to exercise a close surveillance of its citizens. We have looked already at the keeping and analysis of records for police work and for electioneering. IT is used quite innocuously to maintain membership records for societies, charities and book clubs, to record books issued by public libraries and so on. As a by-product, it would be possible to construct an interest-profile of an individual to reveal inclinations towards what those in power currently consider to be subversive. The publication of 'dangerous' books and magazines could even be encouraged so that they could be used as bait.

Our enthusiastic use of credit cards to pay for petrol, train and air tickets, restaurant meals and hotel accommodation leaves an electronic trail that could be used to trace our movements. Growing traffic congestion may well lead to the introduction of toll charges for the use of city streets, motorways, bridges and tunnels; and cars could be fitted with automatic responders to identify their owners, and perhaps their drivers also, in order to debit the corresponding bank accounts. Cars that failed to make an acceptable response would be stopped by the traffic police. There is little to fear, except bankruptcy, when these interceptions relate only to payment, but such a system could easily be extended to constrain the movements of those suspected of a crime, or who have in some other way upset the authorities. Access control is already being used, in the interests of public order, to exclude potential trouble-makers from sports grounds. We need to remain alert and sceptical about the way those in power choose to define 'trouble', for it could become a much more widely drawn misdemeanour than drunken hooliganism. IT places an extremely powerful instrument in the hands of any who choose to misuse it. We must always ask about a proposal for surveillance or control by whom ? for what purpose ? under what supervision ?

IT and expert élites

An inevitable consequence of handling information automatically is that access to it becomes limited to competent and authorized users of IT systems. Some public systems will be open to everyone, but not everyone will be able to afford to pay to use them, for selective and comprehensive information services cannot be cheap. Others will not be equipped by their experience or education to master the access procedures, or to understand the significance of the services on offer: they will neither know their needs nor how to satisfy them. Yet others, and they may well be the majority, will not want to spoil their heedless leisure with dry analyses of dusty facts.

Those who will benefit most will be the eager, the ambitious and the already well informed. IT may be socially divisive, making the information-rich even richer, widening the gulf between them and the information-poor. Unfortunately, those who are poor in information will often be those who are also deprived economically and educationally, and who are most in need of whatever benefits better information might bring. This is no new phenomenon: even books, and before them manuscripts, favoured the powerful and the literate. The developing use of IT is, nevertheless, widening the division at a pace too rapid for the customary processes of human and social adjustment. C. P. Snow introduced the phrase 'the two cultures' to mark the gulf between those who are at home with science and the rest [62]: a yet wider social and political gulf exists between the concerned and informed minority and the feckless majority who neither know nor care to know.

One social division of special importance concerns the role of expert advisers in government[8, 20, 50, 67]. In Britain, the tenure of a minister is brief, and only rarely can he or she hope to master the entire range of business covered by their department. Inevitably they rely on experts, whether public servants or private consultants. As the affairs of government become more complex and technical the experts make increasingly subtle and elaborate analyses. They use the modelling methods of IT, and these can generate unexpected results. In pursuit of greater realism it is natural to increase the number of factors brought into account, but then the behaviour of the model system – especially the dynamic phenomena that accompany changing conditions – quickly passes beyond our unaided powers of understanding. Few ministers are able to challenge what their experts tell them; most face the dilemma that to reject expert advice is irrational, but to accept it is to surrender their authority. The essence of political behaviour is freedom of choice, plus the practical reconciliation of conflicting interests. The last thing any minister wants is professional advice which points unambiguously in an iron-bound way to one uniquely best solution.

A shift in power towards an expert élite and away from ministers and members of representative assemblies (and so, indirectly, away from the electorate) could be the most significant social consequence of using IT. More than three centuries ago, Francis Bacon warned that 'Nothing doth more hurt in a state than that cunning men pass for wise'[5]. Fortunately, three remedies are available. First, it is for the people and not the experts to set the questions and determine the criteria by which solutions will be evaluated. It is most important that this should be done, for if we do not establish clear guidelines then our experts will charge ahead in hot pursuit of the asocial, value-free and charmless objectives of efficiency, economy and elegance by which they judge each other.

Second, the answers given by experts, however eminent, must never be swallowed whole; a robust scepticism about the emperor's new clothes is always in order. Only the naive suppose that experts must always agree, and that they differ only when they are biassed or corrupt. Raw data can usually support a number of different interpretations. We have to live with conflicting expert advice, and take uncertain decisions whose consequences we monitor and correct before they carry us too far down a wrong path.

Third, advice should never be taken from one school of expertise alone: a wise minister will employ a rival school to ensure that alternatives are exposed and evaluated. This, indeed, could become the most socially valuable function of the special-interest pressure groups. However, when such a group, or any citizen or small organization, faces a government department or a large commercial organization, unfairness can arise from the great inequality of the resources available to commission expert advice. Occasionally, also, the field is dominated by a few 'establishment' experts who are able to argue from data which are not available to the public. Criticism is costly, especially where computer modelling has to be used, and I believe that the appropriate opposing group should be given access to the government's data and its computer facilities[50]. The problem would be to persuade ministers to do this for the proposals they favour, and not just for those they wish to see rejected.

Substantive discussions of major issues already take place between government departments and other large bodies, such as industrial groups, professional institutions and trades unions. The sequestering of vital economic and statistical data within the IT systems of these large organizations favours the drift towards corporatism by reducing the ability of democratically elected representatives to influence or even to challenge the formulation of policy. This trend has been much discussed in America in the particular context of the 'military-industrial complex'. The preoccupation of governments with national defence, and with the transient military advantages offered by advances in technology, has both stimulated and distorted the development of IT. In Britain, too large a proportion of the resources allocated to research and development, both public and private, has been diverted to short-term defence objectives rather than to the long-term needs of industry. But, it must be admitted that few know what those needs actually are.

The use of IT by expert advisers immensely enhances their role in the determination of public policy. We need not succumb to the neurotic fantasies of 'conspiracy theory' – the experts can be assumed to have benign intentions. Nevertheless, they do form an élite able to influence the tiny group of white, affluent, elderly, mostly males who take the final decisions. IT specialists – system analysts, programmers, operators and maintenance engineers – constitute an élite within this élite, and the ubiquity of automatic information and control systems has given them great powers of disruption or blackmail. So far, as is normal for the technically minded, they have shown little interest in seeking to flex their political muscles in order to influence the conduct of public affairs. But, their potential must remain attractive to those who might wish to mobilize them to achieve political ends.

More immediately troublesome is the withdrawal of ordinary men and women from participation in public life. Infrequent elections and the perceived political influence of large corporations and of noisy pressure groups have bred a sense of impotence and frustration that leads to alienation and apathy. Nor is this countered by the greatly enhanced flows of news and information emerging in the press and on television. Everyone knows that government departments and other large bodies employ public relations professionals who pasteurize their product to ensure that its consumption poses no risk to their employers' political health. Everyone knows that the media employ the meretricious skills of advertising to paint attractive faces on the images they create. Advertising has diminished the credibility of the information which is put before the public. Oddly enough, IT's very power to gather and process vast amounts of public information, and to select and present a chosen but tiny fraction of it as if it were the whole, may end by engendering habits of inattention and scornful disbelief.

Postscript

The industrialized democracies of the West have grown to sizes and complexities that place a premium on the organization of people, traffic, goods and services. The self-regulating mechanisms of government which served simpler communities cannot meet the needs of our intricate and integrated social systems; their problems lie beyond the simple remedies understood by lay governors. Our societies can now be managed only by professionals using skills and machines which most of us neither possess nor understand. Professionals are specialists, and we must take care not to allow ourselves to be misled by their suboptimal solutions, which benefit only the limited range of activity in which an individual expert is competent. And with the emphasis being placed on 'expert systems' we must resolutely reject the excuse 'the system hasn't been programmed to do that'. Unfortunately, the social sciences are not advanced enough to guide even their specialists towards acceptable solutions – they model and they muddle, and we must hope to learn from their mistakes. One unfortunate consequence of the capacity of IT systems to handle complexity is that we are tempted to put off the difficult task of desirable simplification.[46]

We face complex problems in part because governments have extended their activities into areas previously left to private persons – to education, medicine, and the succour of the poor. A weak minister can easily become the prisoner of events, entangled in the lush undergrowth of routine business. A strong one can be frustrated by the procedural hurdles and delays inherent in the stately operations of democratic assemblies. The simile of the ship of state is a cliché, but note that the ship in question is no lively speedboat; it is a lumbering oil tanker under-engined and under-ruddered. Those temporarily on the bridge may turn the helm and speed the engines as they please, but it is a very long time before the ship responds to command, and when it does so the manoeuvre may well be too late, too slow, to be effective[41]. Some IT specialists have hoped to improve matters by the application of cybernetics. That word was first used by Ampère to denote the arts of government, although Norbert Wiener re-invented it to refer to the science of automatic control systems. In practical government, both IT and cybernetics are means only; it is agreeing on the choice of ends that we find most troublesome.

Preoccupation with the present and postponement of reform are made worse by the brevity of our electoral cycles. In most Western countries the life of a government is a few years at most, and its effective life is shorter still, for in its latter months the thoughts of ministers turn towards the coming election. In his *Politics*, Aristotle argued for a short period in office in order to limit the damage that a politician could do; but it also limits the good. However, the opportunities afforded to ordinary citizens to participate in government are infrequent and cursory enough not to argue for a longer gap between elections. Our sense of political impotence is strengthened when the IT systems of government departments and large corporations hold the data needed to support analyses. In consequence, most ordinary men and women simply drop out into a condition of fatalistic apathy, leaving political life to the minority who find it rewarding, while they turn to private pastimes where they can make their mark, achieve recognition and be valued for their visible individual contributions.

In the nineteenth century, political power did actually reside in the democratic assemblies where we suppose it to lie; in this century, it has moved to the political parties who choose the ministers. In the next century, will it have moved again and reside in the special-interest groups and major corporations ? IT has not caused these changes, but its political influence would be greatly enhanced by them. On the other hand, IT could provide a defence against them should we decide to use it to disperse and decentralize our activities, to allow government to be devolved to the local level, and yet remain effective and coordinated. Pressure groups are less impressive around the parish pump where everyone knows and understands the public interest, and the private motives and personalities involved.

No discussion of the implications of IT for political behaviour can ignore the international scene. The sensitive use of IT could help underdeveloped countries to acquire substitute skills and so accelerate their economic advance. But, the economic consequences for the local workforce, and the cultural consequences for the local community might be unattractive. The distinction between the information-rich and the information-poor applies not only within one nation but also between nations, and the effects of using IT must be to widen the gap between the affluent Western world and the impoverished majority. Economic facts are frail and partial, but the World Bank has predicted differences in average personal income at the end of this century which range from \$10 000 per annum for the 14% who live in the richer countries to \$200 for the 32% who live in the poorer. So large a ratio can neither be ignored nor endured. The principal political problem we face is how to achieve a major redistribution of the products of increasing productivity between nations without shame, and without dictation.

So far, the applications of IT have been directed at economy and efficiency rather than at alleviating human or social ills. Health, education, welfare and overseas aid are all regarded as 'overheads', as burdens which hinder our pursuit of productivity and economic growth. Some commentators appear to believe that social and political problems arise mainly from failures of communication – failures which a quick technological fix, an enthusiastic use of IT, will remedy. To think so is naive; the primary sources of our difficulties are inherent conflicts of interests within and between societies, and IT can do little to help to resolve them.

9

Safe, and pleasant to use

A survey of the implications of information technology runs two risks. First, it may degenerate into a long and tedious list of the ways in which the use of IT bears upon our lives. Second, in seeking to fill the gaps left by enthusiastic advocates it may suggest that the consequences are wholly bad. In this book, beneficial effects are largely taken for granted, for those who design and introduce IT systems are rarely reticent about merits; attention is less often drawn to blemishes. But, we must not forget that adverse consequences could follow from failing to use IT. The intricate pattern of economic and governmental activities that underpins daily life in industrialized countries now depends critically on rapid and effective exchanges of data: without IT that pattern could unravel into chaos. We have already reached the stage where even a temporary failure of a major IT system can have undesirable social and economic repercussions.

When faced with changes we neither understand nor like, we are tempted to choose a scapegoat to bear the blame, and IT has been singled out as the cause of unwelcome social and economic developments that would have happened anyway. Some of these have certainly been accelerated or intensified, but it would be dangerously blinkered and wholly naive to see IT as the principal agent of change. Life is rarely as simple as we suppose.

IT systems perform ancillary functions. No one computes or communicates for its own sake, but only to serve some primary purpose, and no one worried much about telephones, slide rules or typewriters when those were introduced. So, does IT really pose problems large enough, or pressing enough, to claim so much public attention? Dr Johnson once commented: 'No man forgets his original trade; the rights of nations and of kings, sink into questions of grammar if grammarians discuss them'[36]. Those of us whose trade is IT may well have an inflated view of our own importance: the opponents of high technology, or the media, may simply be trying to make our flesh creep, or to distract us from alternative courses that they are preparing us to follow. Perhaps the discussion of human and social consequences is no more than a public relations ploy encouraged by IT manufacturers and installers seeking to convince us – and may be themselves as well – that they take their social responsibilities seriously and are purveying an 'ethical' product.

I think that it is more than this, for few can doubt that, even in its present primitive form, IT provides by far the most powerful means of collecting, storing, analysing and distributing information that men and women have ever had. Or, that information has now so vital a role in knitting together our activities that we are required to think deeply and carefully about the possible consequences of enlarging our use of so influential an instrument. Thinking is not enough; what else can we do? In seeking answers to that question there are traps to be avoided. The first is to invent elevating slogans of an ethical or political nature; for no one takes any notice of them. The second is to look for a quick technical fix; that is the reflex response of most technologists, but such fixes only palliate and introduce their own problems. The complex interactions between IT and human affairs are no more likely to be improved by *ad hoc* tinkering than is an aspirin to cure a brain tumour, although it, too, may offer a temporary but deceptive relief.

Our aim must be not to suppress IT but to make it 'safe, and pleasant to use'. Hence, to avoid distorting or discouraging beneficial proposals, no more controls should be applied than can be shown to be essential, and none at all to areas of use with no social importance; individuals may be allowed to make their own mistakes where these can do no serious harm to others. Control can never be easy, and may soon be impossible, for IT is deeply

enmeshed in the operations of many industries and organizations. To have any hope of success we must act now before the
pattern becomes too firmly set to be altered. The problems that
bedevil prediction add to our difficulties for, obviously enough,
controls must be relevant and firm to be effective; but we must
retain sufficient flexibility to be able to correct or abandon them
should their effects fail to match our expectations. In a democracy, social controls cannot be introduced or removed quickly,
and the planning and commissioning of major IT systems span
periods longer than most freely elected administrations spend in
office.

Professionalism

We tend to think of a profession as a particular occupation, but let
us begin with a distinction. Kipling was wrong, Lalun was not
just 'a member of the most ancient profession in the world' [37],
she was a professional like a professional boxer, working for
money and not for love. Both professionals and the members of a
profession are competent and expect to be paid for it; but belonging to a profession involves something more. The members of a
profession are expected to have a sense of vocation, to be im-
pelled to follow their chosen 'calling' despite every difficulty, and
to do so honestly and responsibly.

Sociologists see the professions as social contrivances designed
to protect individuals and society from incompetence and char-
latanism, from negligence and malpractice. Certainly, the establishment of a professional institution is a well-tried way of
reinforcing the self-control of the experts practising in a defined
field. Protection is especially necessary where – as for IT – the
subject is not well understood by ordinary citizens, and where its
irresponsible practice could have troublesome consequences;
medicine and the law are familiar examples. The accredited
members of a profession are required to meet high standards of
education, training and experience, and to observe written codes
of professional ethics and of good practice. Those who offend can
expect to be disciplined by their peers. In return, they enjoy
above-average social status, and can hope for superior rewards.

The ethical code of a profession is based on the paradigm of a self-employed consultant serving a client who reposes complete confidence in the professional's judgment and integrity, and who relies on his or her willingness to put the job and the client's interest first, and to exclude all third parties. Very few IT specialists, however, are in private practice; most of them are the salaried servants of employers who determine their status and responsibilities, direct their work, and set their own in-house standards and practices. Employee status introduces the employer as a third party, and some salaried jobs pose difficult problems. Can a sales representative really be expected to give unbiassed advice? How feasible actually is it for programmers to refuse to work on projects whose application or design appears to them – but not to their employer – to flout the public interest? Professional people are apt to make claims of altruistic public service with an air of self-conscious superiority that irritates their critics, who see these lofty statements as mere ploys to justify higher status and more cash.

Nevertheless, a professional body can provide independent validation of a practitioner's claim to competence and experience, plus an institutionalized conscience which enjoins a responsible attitude to work. Each of these is especially important in IT, where the suppliers of hardware and software often *define* the user's needs as well as satisfying them. In the Western democracies, competence is regarded as more important than ethics, for it is generally assumed that public or private harm is more likely to be the result of blunders than of malign intent.

The institutions also have a key part to play in helping to allay the public's fear of IT by providing an authoritative voice independent of the trade and the government. They have been less than impressive in this, and must strive to use their role as trustees and developers of an important part of society's stock of knowledge to generate a steady flow of non-trivial information for the media to draw upon. When working with the media, as when advising government, it is necessary to accept the constraints imposed by practical realities, timetables expecially. Public information is the most useful function of a professional society; it is valuable to set standards of qualification which require its members to have mastered current techniques and to have applied them in practice; it is essential to demonstrate that those members are also aware of the wider implications of their work for men, women and for society.

IT has its professional bodies, the British Computer Society and the American Association for Computing Machinery for instance, and in those countries the electrical engineering institutions are also closely involved. To be an effective instrument of social control a profession must be able to grant or withhold, suspend or cancel, the certificate of membership which should be a prerequisite of a licence to practise. This is so in medicine: it is not yet so in IT. As a result many competent and responsible practitioners remain outside; few employers require their staff to be professionally accredited, or reward them when they are. Unless these circumstances change, professionalism will remain a weak form of social control in IT, despite its well-intentioned codes of ethics and good practice.

Public opinion

In a free society, information must flow upwards towards the centres of power as well as downwards to the periphery. The usual media provide for this, but not equally. The outward torrent of news, official announcements and advertising vastly exceeds the publishing of opinions by ordinary men and women, nor is it evident that those who are given the opportunity to answer back are as ordinary, as typical, as they purport to be.

Even so, cogent statements of public opinion to central and local authorities and to company boards occasionally influence their actions. As a last resort, electors and shareholders can 'throw the rascals out'. If our opinions are to be taken seriously they must be well informed, and that is no easy matter. IT has been presented as being too difficult for most of us to hope ever to comprehend; but being difficult is no excuse for not trying, it is rather an incentive to try harder. Only professionals need to master the detail; a broad understanding of how IT systems work and what they can do is well within the capacity of most of us.

The imagined obscurity and consequent mistrust of IT are part of a larger suspicion of science and high-technology. A poll conducted for *New Scientist* in 1985 showed that three-quarters of the British public thought that science was dangerous. Asked which professions gave them a feeling of confidence, 57% answered medicine (a previous poll in the USA gave 46%), and only 19% had any confidence in scientists (USA 38%). However, a mere 13% nominated politicians (USA 13% also), and only 6% voted for journalists (USA 18%). Clearly, there is a large confidence gap, but these results do not suggest that the media are likely to be able to bridge it. The press prints newsy snippets, and television has largely abandoned education for entertainment in its obsessive pursuit of pictures and ratings. The explosion of scientific knowledge during this century has overwhelmed the ordinary citizen, and communication is seriously impeded by the use of an impenetrable jargon, garnished for IT with a liberal handful of meaningless acronyms which reinforce the general impression that, rather than explaining themselves to people, IT experts prefer talking to machines in code.

Somehow the aims and objectives of science and technology must be brought into the domain of public discussion, and receive as much attention as, say, crime or sport. That will not happen unless the IT profession acts more energetically to inform public opinion than it has so far attempted. IT is not alone in neglecting this public duty, other high-tech professions have been no less remiss. Nor will every professional find this task congenial.

I am convinced that the professional institutions concerned with computing, telecommunications and electronics have important and inescapable duties to enlarge the public's understanding of IT. They must make substantial and sustained efforts to work together, with the media and with the agencies of further and adult education to mount attractive well-balanced presentations designed to kill off the stereotypes put forward as the unacceptable face of high technology. To be attended to, these programmes must scrupulously avoid any hint of condescension, any suggestion of propaganda. Ideally, the pressure to inform the public should come from the institutions' own members, but if it does not then the government should oblige the institutions to act.

Give and take will be necessary on both sides, and the more

unworldly members of the profession will have to accept that the commercial imperatives of journalism conflict with their purist ideals of professionalism with a capital P. Journalists have to capture their reader's attention in the first sentence, or they will not be read. They know that what does this are 'human interest' stories of personalities and conflicts which austere professionals regard as entirely irrelevant. Journalists also know that they have to simplify and overstate to the very edge of distortion, raising probabilities to the level of certainties. A supercilious disdain for this huckstering will not change the rules of the game; the professional institutions must learn how to use the media to put across what they want to say. But, they must first decide what that is!

There must, however, be a preliminary process of education within the IT profession itself. Most of its members are just not interested in wider issues; many prefer to immerse themselves in the endlessly fascinating problems posed by machine systems rather than the less logical, more emotional, responses of men and women. Others despise discussions of social consequences as vague and woolly speculations compared with the crystalline realities of technique. Few of IT's professionals have been prepared by their education or their specialist training to handle human or social themes; they see these as the province of other experts. Most of them work under intense pressure to complete projects whose operational purposes have already been defined; and their employers do not encourage them to sit and think about possible impacts on the world outside their system. Some moves are, however, being made to raise the practice of IT above its beginnings as a craft skill. At the Massachusetts Institute of Technology, for example, students of computing and telecommunications also take courses in the humanities and the social sciences – although many of them see these as unnecessary evils which deflect them from their prime objective, and which may add another year of undergraduate work. Despite all these doubts and difficulties, we must insist that all who aspire to full professional status be required to demonstrate that they have studied and are alert to the external consequences of their work.

A good general education for all citizens offers the only lasting protection against the misuse of technology. Putting a microcomputer into every school is neither good nor bad in itself; much depends on whether they are used to encourage the development of critical and creative skills, or merely seen as a means of instilling a mechanical competence that employers will require. Learning about the technology itself can dispel the gloomier fears expressed by half-instructed commentators. Learning some history can set the events of yesterday and today against a broader background. Learning a foreign language can help us to see the world through the eyes of a different culture, and is particularly valuable for native speakers of English, for it has become the principal language of the theory and practice of IT, and must therefore be imbued with its presuppositions.

Governments of all persuasions are likely to agree on the need for more and better public information about IT, for there is no political advantage in allowing ignorance to breed fear. As a first step, political parties and members of assemblies must themselves be convinced that the development and use of IT cannot be safely dismissed with a cursory nod. Here is a dog that needs more than an absent-minded pat on the head, for it may turn surly and bite. But, politicians move only when pushed, and in a system with frequent elections their prime concern is to be re-elected. It is not cynical to say this, for politicians who fail to be elected lose all power. The issues that they perceive to have the most votes value attract their closest attention, and the route to political action lies through the mobilization of public opinion.

Pressure groups

Faction is the older word but has acquired overtones of unscrupulousness; factions and pressure groups are alike in energetic, single-minded pursuit of their aims. Recognizing that only large armies can hope to advance on broad fronts, they concentrate their attack on a few clear objectives, and that can make them seem unbalanced. Their purpose is to enhance and maintain public awareness of specific problems, and to build up a countervailing expertise to challenge the arguments put forward in support of unwelcome new proposals.

Groups concerned with the conservation and protection of the

environment are familiar examples, which press their case relent-
lessly with an acute awareness of what will make a headline. That
is most readily achieved by dramatic opposition: amelioration
and steady improvement are no less important, but much less
newsworthy. Conservation has attracted enough attention to
have given rise to 'Ecology' or 'Green' parties. The older political
parties have more broadly based programmes and until they
accept that IT has become a substantial matter of public concern
and include it among their policies it will not be treated very
seriously.

Some non-party groups are also active in politics, for instance
those concerned with nuclear disarmament and with civil liberties. Each has an indirect involvement with IT: the first through
its key role in the design and guidance of weapon systems; the
second by way of issues of privacy, personal surveillance, police
work and national security. Consumer associations have been
formed to safeguard the rights of customers, and to expose deficiencies in the goods and services provided for them. All of
these pressure groups must take a close and sustained interest in
the development and application of IT: otherwise they could,
quite suddenly, find themselves outflanked.

The uses of IT by employers are the particular concern of the
trade unions. These were set up as pressure groups to protect the
interests of workers with specific skills, or those employed in
certain industries. Rapid changes in industrial organization and
ownership, and in techniques, are presenting the unions with
acute problems, as crafts become obsolete and industries re-
group. These problems are most severe when the employer is a
large multinational corporation supplying a wide range of products which it manufactures or assembles in different countries.
Trade unions remain, nevertheless, the established way for
workers to bring pressure to bear; but established organizations
tend to ossify, and the unions must resist the insidious onset of
rigidity.

It has not been usual to see the churches as pressure groups,
but they are becoming so as the cultural composition of the
populations of Western countries continues to diversify. In Bri-

tain, for example, we can no longer presume that most people are Christians: Jewish, Islamic, Buddhist, Hindu, Sikh, other faiths and none, all claim adherents. No longer is it realistic to assume a common ethical foundation, or a shared set of social aims, values and priorities. So far, however, the impact of religion on the development and use of IT has been negligible: the churches have been slow to develop coherent doctrines covering the secular aspects of life and work in industrial societies.

Voluntary restraint

In principle, it would be possible for the users and suppliers of IT systems and services to agree, without coercion, to moderate their rates of production and application in order to allow more time for human and social adjustment, and to enable sober, independent, assessments to be made of external consequences. But they are likely to do so only if convinced that examining and anticipating potential problems will save them money, or sharpen their competitive edge. A more humane approach to system design does, in fact, offer significant advantages in improved relations with staff and with customers; advantages which, in the longer term, will outweigh the short-term gains won by a head-down drive for efficiency and economy.

Boards of directors have to understand that IT is too vital a component of their companies' future success to be abandoned to the tunnel vision of its specialists. Directors are not yet asking the right questions: on the whole they have been content with pedestrian mechanization when they should be focusing on effectiveness rather than efficiency. Small savings in the costs of routine office work are a mere catch crop: the principal harvest will come from the improved planning, and the better and faster product design, necessary to survive, to compete and to grow. Architects mediate between house builders and customers, understanding both the needs of their clients and the capabilities and constraints of the technology. The corresponding function is lacking in IT, which sorely needs its creative 'system architects'. Looking at some modern commercial buildings, however, does suggest that IT's architects should not be allowed to become too inward-looking a cadre; what we require are amphibians, able to breathe the rarified air of IT, but equally at home in the muddy waters of business.

On the whole, it seems more likely that the rate of introduction of IT will be held back not by self-restraint but by the organized resistance of workers opposing what they feel will make them and their skills redundant. Their tactic has been to attempt to delay the introduction of modern methods until safeguards, transfers to other work, and compensatory awards can be negotiated. That tactic has not always succeeded. IT has transformed newspaper production despite bitter opposition from the printers, with the result that they have lost their jobs to a much smaller number of members of a more accommodating union – and one not confined to printing. It is, however, too facile to stigmatize resisting workers as Luddites; history suggests that technological changes have rarely, if ever, been made with the specific objectives of improving the conditions and increasing the rewards of the labour force.

Government

There are those who play upon the fears which ordinary men and women have of advanced science and technology, fears which have been reinforced by the horrors of nuclear war, and by the Frankenstein threats of genetic engineering. They criticize the pressures of high-technology urban life as unnatural, commending an innocent rusticity. Blinded by a burning sense of conviction, they suppose that a new Garden of Eden could accommodate today's hundreds of millions, and arrogantly assume that we wait only for them to reveal the light in order to yearn for the pleasures, the chores and the diseases of the simple life.

The remedy proposed by these seers for the problems of IT is a simple one – total prohibition. Certainly, the world existed for many centuries without IT, and many parts of it still do so; and it would not be absolutely impossible to abandon its use altogether. But, such a course has no chance of being adopted. IT systems are now so pervasive throughout industry, commerce and government, their provision and operation involve so much money and so many people, and the problems of reverting to manual methods are so horrendous, that the likelihood of any democratic government winning agreement to abolish the use of IT is zero. And no non-democratic government is likely to divest itself of so powerful an instrument of social control. IT may be an agent of change but, like all revolutionaries, once established it strongly favours maintaining the status quo.

Governments are very large users of IT systems and major employers of specialists, and their own internal codes of conduct and practice set an example for others. The British government, for instance, could require its staff to acquire professional qualifications, and reward them for doing so, but so far it has not. Governments also carry out, or finance, research and development; and exert a strong influence over the scope and scale of teaching. Many government systems operate in highly sensitive areas – taxation and health, defence and public order, for example – and there ought to be a very much more general discussion of such projects before they are launched. I believe that any new project in the public domain should be presented for open consideration and, where substantial objections are voiced, should be the subject of a formal public enquiry with independent appraisal. Quite apart from any social consequences, it's our money that will be spent! Established government systems should be subject to random 'audits', not only to ensure financial probity but also to check that the modifications and developments which all systems attract have not introduced undesirable consequences subsequent to initial approval.

Procedures known as 'social impact analysis', or 'technology assessment', have been devised to explore all foreseeable consequences, good as well as bad, in an objective and rational way. America has an 'Office of Technology Assessment' with substantial funds and an expert staff: Britain has no adequate equivalent. But, before rushing into technology assessments, we ought to consider whether we can, in practice, foresee and head off the unpleasant consequences of specific applications of IT. Is prediction really possible in human affairs? Economics and sociology are fearsomely difficult subjects, and we do not yet understand them well enough to be able to make accurate long-range forecasts. Moreover, the development of technology is enlivened by the eruption of novelties which buck the trend. No one could have foreseen the emergence of the transistor, but without its development into cheap and reliable microchips IT would not have achieved the breadth and variety of applications we see today. Attempts to forecast the social and economic impacts of a new technology are also hampered by the fact that many of its more bothersome consequences are unexpected. As Philip Larkin put it: 'Most things are never meant'[38]. Yet side-effects, unintended and unfortunate, unwanted and uncontrolled, are no less painful. Modelling can offer little help, for we rarely know which factors are involved, nor the nature of their interaction.

Again, before launching out into a technology assessment, we have to agree which social objectives are to be sought and which avoided, and to decide over what timescale the effects are to be evaluated. Objectives involve values and these, with the timing and the scope of the investigation, raise major matters of policy about which the different political parties and private interests will hold diverse views. And, many human and social gains and losses cannot be quantified in any meaningful way; some attempts to compute 'social costs' have an extremely contrived air, and convince no one but their authors. Most troublesome of all is our ignorance of the causes and the development of social change under political and economic constraints. We are forced to make do with empirical correlations derived from inadequate data. Computer models can help with the mechanics of calculation, and the analysis of equilibrium situations, but our ability to program them to handle the dynamic aspects of transitions in social and economic systems remains to be demonstrated. Nor can the development of a satisfactory computer model be cheap or quick.

The practical impossibility of making a complete study, plus the high cost of making an adequate one, explain why so few assessments have been made; and few indeed will be made unless legislation so requires. Moreover, the results point only to probabilities, and may indicate adverse consequences where none would in fact arise. Even so, we must strive to develop technology assessment, and make it a legal requirement, if only to counter the distressing tendency of the champions of new IT systems to utter a variety of soothing statements, for example:

- our critics are basing their alarmist remarks on mere speculation, for the alleged risks have not been proved to be serious (true, the future does not yet exist);
- any disadvantages would be limited and minor compared with the massive economic benefits to society as a whole (so the unlucky few ought to be happy to suffer for the fortunate many);
- any problems would only be temporary, for the rapid advance of technology will provide ways to reduce the harm (but tomorrow's jam may have its own bitter taste, and quick fixes often have unpalatable side-effects);
- should the social consequences prove to be unexpectedly adverse, the government will act to protect society by legislation (eventually, perhaps, but incompletely and in arrears);
- give us time, we're slowly getting it right (Fig. 5).

Those who prefer a broad sweep to their history, rather than recalcitrant details, claim to discern the operation of a 'technological imperative' – an impersonal force driving us ever forward into increasingly complex applications of science. In our context, it is no more than a vivid label for the massive economic power of

Fig. 5. A typical soothing statement. (*Courtesy of Bill Tidy.*)

the IT industry, which relies on restless innovation and expansion as it seeks its own commercial goals, and feeds the military ambitions of its larger customers. There is no organized conspiracy here, merely the piecemeal pursuit of private advantage. However, the massive size of that industry – hardware, software and services – and the importance of its applications are such that we must take pains to ensure, by government action if necessary, that it never becomes a monopoly, public or private, national or international.

Legislation is the ultimate sanction that a government can use, but as Gibbon pointed out: 'the operation of the wisest laws is imperfect and precarious. They seldom inspire virtue, they cannot always restrain vice'[27]. Nor can we be certain that a new law will be so wisely drawn that it will not unintentionally create its own unwelcome phenomena. It would be exceptionally difficult to frame a satisfactory law to regulate IT, because its potential is still largely untapped, and its techniques continue to develop rapidly with no early limit in sight. Any law we draft today would almost certainly prove to be too rigid, and preclude or distort future developments of acknowledged social value. Moreover, it could be totally by-passed by unforeseen advances in technology. Thus, a law which sought to protect privacy by prohibiting the exchange of personal information between separate organizations across frontiers would be frustrated by the development of satellite links which, as a by-product, offered direct and uncontrolled access to foreign data havens. An ample supply of obsolete laws exists and needs no supplementation.

These considerations argue for enacting only those legal controls that are absolutely essential to protect the public; and for that minimum to be expressed in terms of broad principles rather than technical detail. In my view, the most useful legislation that could be enacted would be to require certain categories of IT system to be designed and implemented by licensed practitioners only: other less-sensitive projects would remain open to all. Licences to practise would be granted only to properly qualified members of the profession, who would then be the only persons legally entitled to work in such areas as those that affect personal privacy or liberty, national defence or the safety of life.

Obviously, the qualifying bodies would have to satisfy the government that they were enforcing codes of professional ethics and good practice; and a few heads would have to roll *'pour encourager les autres'*.

There are, however, areas of use where the law may need to be changed or supplemented to cover offences specific to IT. New legal problems are presented by hacking that causes annoyance but no loss; again, when an IT system fails problems arise over the assignment of damages between the manufacturer of the hardware, the producer of the software, the programmers, the suppliers of data and the operators. The application of copyright law to software shows that the law need not be solely negative; it can offer protection in order to encourage economic growth.

In Britain, the prospects for passing new laws to control IT are not bright; we are not likely to be able to muster the necessary amount of political will. Members of parliament recognize an unpopular subject when they see one, and the parliamentary timetable is always overcrowded. The subject is too technical to inspire great flights of oratory, or even to make the headlines. Political action always follows the event, and the short-serving administrations of Western countries follow the rule 'crisis first, cure later'. However, no adverse effect is inevitable; we can still take charge of our fate, but unless we do so we could drift into disaster.

We face a future in which, although IT will play a major part, its development will probably be allowed to continue along the opportunistic path that it has followed so far. This *laissez-faire* approach is favoured by right-wing governments in the democracies, for it avoids the need to act, assumes that users and suppliers know their own requirements better than any government official, and is content to leave international competition to generate whatever thrust is necessary to drive development and exploitation. Social and economic affairs remain free from governmental control or intervention; there is no set course and no helmsman; no countervailing force operates in the 'public interest' to restrain the massive commercial drive of the IT industry. Such a government limits itself to setting minimum standards, and to punishing those clumsy enough to be caught *in flagrante delicto*.

None of this would matter if we could assume that we have established processes that maximize the social gains and share the externalities – the social costs. One alternative is to attempt to steer the development of IT along paths expected to be socially and economically beneficial. Three questions arise. First, who exactly are the 'we' who will do the steering? Presumably the government, for no one else could exercise the authority or claim a mandate. Second, who will predict and assess the future consequences of alternative courses of action or inaction? No one yet knows how to do so. Third, how can we hope to agree about the pace of development, the directions to be followed, or the destinations to be sought? Unity of purpose is a rare social phenomenon, more common in war than in peace. Despite these difficulties, this approach appeals to those on the left-hand side of the political spectrum. It appeals also to the tender-hearted who occupy the greener regions of that spectrum, but they, luxuriating in fervent expressions of objection, often forget that politics is the art of the possible and achieve little more than emotional relief.

The international dimension

When reviewing the human and social problems posed by IT we do well to reflect that they are wholly insignificant when compared with the great questions of population growth, resource exhaustion, industrial pollution and nuclear war, which dominate international agenda. Each of these is exacerbated by our use of high technology. Population growth, for example, derives more from the survival of a larger number of infants to child-bearing age than from increased fecundity. Thanks to improved medical techniques a large proportion of the world's population is now under 15 years of age, and will soon be making its own contribution to the rate of increase.

IT itself has done little to increase the population, but it is to some extent responsible for the rising expectations which mean that by AD 2000 the world's population may well demand 10 times as much per capita in goods and services as today's consumers. The problems posed by population growth and rising expectations are most acute in the underdeveloped nations of the so-called Third World, and in the impoverished ones of the 'Fourth World'. Taken together these are the homelands of most of us who live on planet Earth. IT has little to offer them: indeed, by promoting productivity through automation, and by requiring skilled operators of high quality, it may erode their principal economic advantage of cheap labour. Should that happen the economic gap will widen yet further as the rich get richer and the poor get children.

The nations of the Third and Fourth Worlds are mainly agricultural, and there seems to be a presumption in the West that their economic destinies should follow the same evolutionary path as Europe, Japan and the USA. Why that should be is not clear. Certainly, those industrial countries have followed roughly parallel courses, and their economies now overlap and interlock. They are all caught up in the same web of worldwide communications, and when one stumbles the rest react instantly and anxiously. The linkages between them have grown piecemeal, and the system has not been specifically designed for stability. It is a strange policy to seek to tie the non-industrial societies into this network at a time when the post-industrial ones may find it prudent to loosen their own connections to it.

Moreover, the nature of manufacturing has changed irrevocably since Britain's Industrial Revolution, and there is decreasing scope for absorbing workers displaced from agriculture. Ready-made Western solutions, evolved in wholly different circumstances are likely to be seen as an alien implant and resisted as a form of 'technological colonialism'. Some have, therefore, suggested that it would be better for the underdeveloped countries to adopt less exotic methods of working which require more labour and less skill. That, too, has more than a hint of paternalism and, although these alternative technologies could promote economic development, the rate of growth would be much less rapid than those being achieved as the West presses ahead with IT. The economic gap would continue to widen at an increasing rate.

Much more thinking needs to be done before anyone rushes in

to treat these troubles with a dose of IT. Nor are the Third and Fourth Worlds homogeneous entities; there are many individual nations, each with its own culture and traditions, each having its own special difficulties, and each requiring to be treated with dignity and respect. Their enormous problems dwarf our technological remedies; but we must take care not to decline into discouragement and despair. The problems are pressing, but their solutions are inescapably long-term; and that presents difficulties related to continuity of policy in the Western democracies. Perhaps the most useful contribution we could make would be to formulate and agree bipartisan policies under which we offer free education to as many students from Third and Fourth World countries as can benefit from graduate courses, so that they may return to develop solutions that match the culture, and respond sensitively to the conditions, of their countries.

Postscript

During the last century the development and exploitation of technology was expected to make us all healthier, wealthier, happier and wiser. The First World War killed that Pollyanna optimism, and in reaction we risk sinking into apathy as we await an inevitable doom. With G. K. Chesterton, I do not believe in a fate that falls on men, however they act, but in one that falls on them unless they act. Conscious action is now required of us, for nothing in the long slow haphazard stages of our biological evolution has prepared us to flourish in the non-natural world which IT is helping to create. In the course of evolution our ancestors *reacted* to changes which had already altered their environments. Today, we have to *anticipate* changes in ours, and we must also make sure that the institutions of our society are flexible enough to accommodate them.

Change is the norm in human affairs, and our problem is to achieve painless, controlled, constructive transitions from where we are to where we want to be. What we are most likely to see are *post hoc* attempts to ameliorate the worst effects of high technology, attempts which risk the verdict 'too little, too late'. But, we dare not do nothing, for then IT's new products and services will insidiously encapsulate us in individual cocoons as education, news, entertainment and even work move out of the public domain and on to our domestic video screens[25, 54]. Such a trend would greatly weaken the cohesion of society; divide and rule is an old maxim, and those who then controlled the sources of public information would be better placed to rule than anyone has ever been before.

The provision of optical cable and satellite links to individual homes will allow a massive multiplication of television channels. Their specialization into news, sport, education and various kinds of trivial pursuit will offer a seemingly wide choice – but one between predetermined possibilities. The result could be to contract rather than to expand our range of interests, as we watch only the sports we enjoy and ignore the news that bores us. We could be drenched with electronic information but be singularly ill informed. I have a nightmare vision of a vegetable populace neatly planted out before its screens eating its mass-produced convenience meals, and absorbing an equally bland pabulum of convenience information supplied over the national networks. Of course, that need never happen; but can we be sure, or even hopeful, that the rest of IT will not suffer the fate of colour television – degraded to carry newsy titbits, soap operas, juvenile quiz games and infantile advertisements. We have a most unfortunate knack of inventing a splendid technology and then perverting it to petty ends.

I admit that this is a élitist view, and one based on old-fashioned values: but we do not live in a vacuum and if we do not form our own explicit value-judgements we leave ourselves open to a subliminal acceptance of the implicit values or at least the aims, of the programme makers whose outpourings fill the channels. At this early stage of IT they are hag-ridden by immediacy and driven towards urgent commercial objectives, with no sense of any longer or broader perspective. Perhaps we should rejoice that this is so, and that all we have to complain of is inanity and incoherence; for IT could as well be used to support a single-minded tyranny as a feckless consumerism.

To judge by the public discussion of IT, we appear to have lost our nerve. Offered a powerful tool we fret peevishly about what it may do *to* us, when we should be planning what it can do *for* us.

What will actually happen will depend on what men and women decide to do, the choice is ours, and we still have time to make it; but in doing so we should remember Agnes Allen's observation that: 'Almost everything is easier to get into than to get out of'[21].

So far, IT has had little effect on our lives, and the discussion of its possible impact has been confined to a small fraction of those who work in the field. They tend to assume that uninterrupted and rapid technical development will continue and, accepting a mild form of the technological imperative, never question that whatever can be done will be done. Some of them paint naive pictures of a leisured society in which tireless robots do all the work, and intelligent ones do all the worrying. It may be no accident that such visions emphasize the important role to be played by technologists as the wise and rational governors of society. But, these matters are too important to be left to a desultory debate between a few experts. IT really does raise serious issues which can, and which should, be examined by everyone. In Lancelot Hogben's words: 'no society is safe in the hands of so few clever people'[32]. Neither they, nor our machines, can relieve us of the uncomfortable duty of thinking for ourselves.

IT: summary agenda of aims for all concerned

1. Universities and research laboratories

1.1. Conduct research free from external misdirection in pursuit of short-range objectives set by industry or the state (8.3, below).
1.2. Develop an improved theoretical base for cooperative multi-processor computing in parallel and network systems.
1.3. Inform the professions and the media fully and frequently about research in progress and its implications.

2. The IT industry

2.1. Continue free to develop and produce hardware, software and services to meet commercial objectives of own choosing, subject only to the trading controls generally applied to protect the rights of customers.
2.2. Participate in, and help to fund, the development of improved methods of technology assessment (4.4 and 8.5, below).

3. Users of IT systems

3.1. Continue free to develop and operate IT systems at will, scrupulously observing legislation to protect privacy, and subject only to the controls generally applied to maintain the rights of customers and employees.
3.2. Top management and governing boards: learn enough about IT to exercise firm strategic control over their organization's use of

it, in order to redirect projects (too narrowly conceived by specialists) which could damage their customer or industrial relations (4.5, below).

3.3. Take potential consequences into account when designing systems, accepting some extra cost, delay and loss of efficiency where necessary to mitigate adverse effects (4.5, below).

3.4. Consult employees and customers liable to be affected by new proposals before these have been finalized, and while they can be modified to meet valid objections.

3.5. Provide adequately for on-the-job training and retraining to meet changed and changing circumstances (8.8, below).

4. Professional institutions

4.1. Raise and broaden the levels of education, training and experience required for qualification.

4.2. Apply disciplinary rules strictly and effectively, suspend or cancel licence to practice of members who contravene codes of ethics or practice (8.9, below).

4.3. Commission top-level interdisciplinary group, including advisors from other professions, to evaluate the likely personal, social, economic and cultural consequences of specific uses of IT: promulgate and act on its findings.

4.4. Lead the development of improved methods and administration for technology assessment of IT systems (2.2 above; 8.5, below).

4.5. Urge members acting as designers or consultants to advise clients to rate effectiveness and human relations above efficiency and economy, and to press the advantages to users themselves of maximizing working flexibility, use of skills, and a sense of achievement when operating IT systems – recognizing that people are assets, machinery is only a cost (3.2 and 3.3 above).

4.6. Accept as a primary duty the need to keep the public properly informed, establishing a standing group of senior members charged to generate a regular flow of comprehensible material about the nature and implications of current developments in IT (5.1, below).

4.7. Establish a panel of members available to provide rapid, authoritative responses to (always) urgent enquiries by the media (5.1, below).

4.8. Establish and foster close liaison with government departments, ministers and members of legislative assemblies.

5. The media

5.1. Recognize the importance of allaying unnecessary alarm about IT by publishing well-balanced, non-sensational, news and background material about personalities, developments and implications, drawing on information made available by the professional institutions (4.6 and 4.7 above).

6. Individual citizens

6.1. Study to understand enough about IT to participate effectively in discussions affecting its future – and ours.

6.2. Refuse to be overawed by illusory accuracy or apparent prestige of information issuing from IT systems, or to be scared by naive and premature claims for artificial intelligence.

6.3. As customers: protest insistently and cogently to companies and officials using IT about errors, infringement of rights, loss of services, junk mail and so on, adamantly refusing to accept alleged inflexibility of IT as a glib excuse.

6.4. Remain eternally vigilant.

7. Pressure groups

7.1. Keep abreast of developments in IT, and all extensions of its use.

7.2. Develop or recruit expertise to be able to present valid objections, and offer constructive alternatives, to proposals expected to have unwelcome consequences.

7.3. Trade unions: adopt flexible approaches to changes in organization, working conditions, job definitions and skill boundaries, for all will be affected by IT.

8. Government

8.1. Act to enable, not to constrain.

8.2. Set an example of the open and responsible use of IT in its own systems.

8.3. Fund undirected long-term research into the theoretical base of IT (1.1 above).

8.4. Maximize 'technology transfer' by positive action to diffuse knowledge acquired in military R & D; do not just hope for spin-off.

8.5. Fund the development of improved methods of technology assessment (4.4 above).

8.6. Promote the development of networking standards for worldwide operation in order to boost international trade, especially in information services exported over telecommunication links.

8.7. Stimulate the growth of remote 'work centres' in order to reduce depopulation and increase employment opportunities in rural areas.

8.8. Promote development of interactive video disc and other IT techniques applicable to on-the-job and in-the-home education, training and retraining (3.5, above).

8.9. Define and list sensitive applications, especially those with safety or security implications, and for these (but for them only):

(a) restrict their design to qualified professionals holding a valid licence to practise, applying this measure rigorously to government staff and work (4.2, above);

(b) require proposals for new or amended systems to be widely published with adequate notice, and public enquiries to be held if reasonable objections are recorded;

(c) require independent audits of performance within stated periods, and the results to be published.

8.10. Set an example in its own work of effective observance of privacy legislation.

8.11. Act wherever necessary to prevent the emergence of a monopoly in telecommunications, in computing, or in their synergy – IT.

8.12. Review the need to legislate to discourage hacking.

8.13. Recognize the transient value of 'relevance' in education; direct attention to education for increased leisure; emphasize the key importance of developing and retaining life-long 'trainability'.

8.14. Work with international organizations to examine how IT can be most relevantly used to alleviate the economic problems of the countries of the so-called Third and Fourth Worlds.

References

1. Ada, Countess of Lovelace (1842). Notes on 'Sketch of the Analytical Engine Invented by Charles Babbage, by J. Menabrea'. In *Charles Babbage and his Calculating Engines*, ed. P. Morrison and J. Morrison, Dover (1961).
2. Airy, W. (ed.) (1896). *Autobiography of Sir George Biddell Airy K.C.B.*, Cambridge University Press.
3. Alfvén, H. (1968) [under the pen name Olof Johannesson] *The Great Computer*, Gollancz .
4. Audit Commission (1985) *Computer Fraud Survey*, HM Stationery Office.
5. Bacon, F. (1625). Essay XXII: Of cunning. In *Essays*.
6. Barnaby, F. (1982). Microelectronics in war. In *Microelectronics in Society*, ed. G. Friedrich and A. Schaff, Pergamon.
7. Bell, D. (1976). *The Coming of Post-Industrial Society*, Penguin Books.
8. Benveniste, G: (1973). *The Politics of Expertise*, Croom Helm.
9. Berger, P. L. & Luckman, T. (1971). *The Social Construction of Reality*. Penguin Books.
10. Boden, M. A. (1977) *Artificial Intelligence and Natural Man*, The Harvester Press.
11. *Book of Common Prayer*, Article xxiv.
12. Bowden, B. V. (ed.) (1953). *Faster than Thought*, Pitmans.
13. Brandeis, Louis, D., Justice (1928). Quoted in *HEWS Report: Records, Computers and the Rights of Citizens*, US Department of Health, Education and Welfare.
14. Brouwer, J. Quoted in *The Coming Clash: The Impact of International Corporations on the Nation State*, by H. Stephenson, Weidenfeld & Nicolson (1972).
15. Burke, E. (1790). *Reflections on the Revolution in France*.
16. Carlyle, T. (1850). *Latter Day Pamphlets*. No. 1: *The Present Time*.
17. Chesterton, G. K. (1925). *The Everlasting Man*.

18. Clarke, A. C. (1962). *Profiles of the Future*, Harper & Row.
19. Cole, H. S. D., Freeman, C., Johoda, M. & Pavitt, K. L. R: (eds) (1973). *Thinking about the Future*, Sussex University Press.
20. Cross, N., Elliott, D. & Roy, R. (eds.) (1974). *Man-made Futures*, Hutchinson.
21. Dickson, P. (1978). *The Official Rules*, Arrow Books.
22. Doswell, R. & Simons, G. L. (1987). *Fraud and Abuse of IT Systems*, NCC Publications.
23. Emerson, R. W. (1883). *Ode to W. H. Channing*.
24. Encel, S., Marstrand, P. K. & Page, W. (eds.) (1975). *The Art of Anticipation*, Martin Robertson.
25. Forster, E. M. (1909). The machine stops. In *Oxford and Cambridge Review*. Reprinted in *The New Collected Short Stories*, by E. M. Forster, Sidgwick and Jackson (1985).
26. Galbraith, K. (1977). *The Age of Uncertainty*, BBC Publications.
27. Gibbon, E. (1787). *The Decline and Fall of the Roman Empire*.
28. Gilbert, W. S. (1885). *The Mikado*.
29. Harman, C. How to fight the new technology. From a Socialist Workers' Pamphlet (1979) reproduced in *The Microelectronics Revolution*, ed. T. Forester, Basil Blackwell (1980).
30. Hicks, J. (1979). *Causality in Economics*, Blackwell.
31. Hofstadter, D. R. (1979). *Gödel, Escher, Bach*, Penguin Books.
32. Hogben, L. (1963). *Science in Authority*, Allen & Unwin.
33. Hopkins, H. (1973). *The Numbers Game*, Secker & Warburg.
34. Hudson, L. (1968). *Frames of Mind*, Methuen.
35. Hutchins, R. M. (1970). *The Learning Society*, Penguin Books.
36. Johnson, S. (1781). *Lives of the English Poets*.
37. Kipling, R. (1888), On the City Wall. In *Soldiers Three*, Macmillan (1965).
38. Larkin, P. (1974). *High Windows*. Faber.
39. Lighthill, J. (1972) *Artificial Intelligence: Report to the Science Research Council*, S.E.R.C.
40. Lindop, Sir Norman (1978). *Report of the Committee on Data Protection*, HM Stationery Office.
41. McHale, J. (1976). *The Changing Information Environment*, Paul Elek.
42. Marx, K. & Engels, F. (1848). *The Communist Manifesto*.
43. Mead, M. (1963). Why is education obsolescent? in *The Teacher and the Taught*, ed. R. Gross, Dell Publishing Co.
44. Meadows, D. H., Meadows, D. L., Randers, J. & Behrens, W. W: (1974) *The Limits to Growth*, Pan Books.
45. Mesarovic, M. & Pestel, E: (1975). *Mankind at the Turning Point*, Hutchinson.
46. Michael, D. N. (1968). *On Coping with Complexity: Planning and Politics*. Daedalus. Reprinted in part in *Information Technology in a Democracy*, ed. A. Westin, Harvard University Press (1971).

47. Michie, D. & Johnston, R. (1985). *The Creative Computer. Machine Intelligence and Human Knowledge*, Viking.

48. Moore, R. (1987). *The Ecodisc*, BBC Enterprises. Reviewed in *New Scientist*, 2 July 1987.

49. Morgenstern, O. (1963). *On the Accuracy of Economic Observations*, 2nd edn, Princeton University Press.

50. Mumford, E. & Sackman, H. (eds.) (1975). *Human Choice and Computers*, North Holland.

51. Neustadt, R. H. (1985). Electronic politics. In *The Information Technology Revolution*, ed. T. Forester, Basil Blackwell.

52. Nilles, J. M. et al. (1976). *The Telecommunications-Transportation Trade-off*, John Wiley.

53. Packard, V. (1957). *The Hidden Persuaders*, David McKay.

54. Pawley, M. (1975). *The Private Future*, Pan Books.

55. Peitgen, H. O. & Richter, P. H. (1986). *The Beauty of Fractals*, Springer-Verlag.

56. Perry, R. (1984). *The Programming of the President*, Aurum Press.

57. Rivers, P. (1974). *Politics by Pressure*, Harrap.

58. Rose, H. & Rose, S. (1970). *Science and Society*, Penguin Books.

59. Sarson, Richard (1987). Three-quarters of a million jobs will go, says report. *The Times*, 31 March.

60. Smith, A. (1987). Quoted in *The Times*, 24 February.

61. Smith, L. P. (1931). *Afterthoughts*. Constable.

62. Snow, C. P. (1969). *The Two Cultures, and a Second Look*. Cambridge University Press.

63. Strachey, C. (1977). In *The Fontana Dictionary of Modern Thought*, p. 124. Fontana.

64. Strassman, P. A. (1985) *Information Payoff: The Transformation of Work in the Electronic Age*, The Free Press.

65. *The Times* (1987). First Leader, 14 April 1987.

66. Weizenbaum, J. (1984). *Computer Power and Human Reason*, Penguin Books.

67. Williams, S. (1985). *A Job to Live*, Penguin Books.

68. Wood, M. (1983). *Introducing Computer Security*, NCC Publications.

69. Yazdani, M. (ed.) (1986). *Artificial Intelligence: Principles and Applications*, Chapman & Hall.

Index

Printed in the United States
By Bookmasters